PRAYERS
THAT ARE
ANSWERED

PRAYERS THAT ARE ANSWERED

BETTY MALZ

Published by
chosen books
Lincoln, Virginia 22078
Distributed by Word Books • Waco, Texas 76703

Library of Congress Cataloging in Publication Data

Malz, Betty.
    Prayers that are answered.

    1. Prayer. 2. Malz, Betty. I. Title.
BV210.2.M32   248'.3   79–24532

ISBN 0–912376–50–3

*This book is dedicated
to my father,
Glenn Perkins.
(You taught me how to pray.)*

also . . .

*I dedicate this book to
everyone who has a prayer
yet unanswered.*

ACKNOWLEDGMENTS

My appreciation to Leñ LeSourd, whose editorial assistance and expertise lifted this manuscript from its rough beginnings to a completed work which I consider to be the result of answered prayer.

God has a thousand ways to work
   Where I can see, not one;
When all my means have reached their end,
   Then His has just begun!

                           (Guyot)

CONTENTS

Introduction   13
1   Prayer for a Mate   15
2   The Answer   32
3   Family Prayer   45
4   Prayer for Wisdom and Guidance   58
5   Prayer for Small Needs   69
6   The One-Word Prayer   79
7   Dangerous Prayer   90
8   The Anonymous Prayer   100
9   A Moving Adventure   112
10 Dialogue with God   125
11 Prayer for the Resistant   139
12 Prayer Warriors   152
13 The Left Hand of God   163

INTRODUCTION

THE TURNING POINT of my life came in 1959 at the Union Hospital in Terre Haute, Indiana. For weeks I had lain there in bed, close to death from a burst appendix and peritonitis. At 5 A.M. on a summer morning, my life functions stopped.

Suddenly I was standing in the direct rays of a radiant yellow light. I realized where I was, for there was no sickness there, and I was suddenly standing erect and physically well. I saw powerful, direct shafts of light coming from the earth, directly to the "throne room" where the great light source originates.

I realized that these shafts were prayers ascending from the earth to the center of all creative power and merging with that great light. One prayer was meaningful. I saw it, and I heard it—one word: "Jesus." It was my father's voice. It asked for nothing, yet it asked for everything. In it was a wish, a desire, a plea. He wished I had not died. It drew me back—down the hill, to the hospital room and back to my bed.

In *My Glimpse of Eternity* I wrote about my "death." But the prayer adventures were just starting. Twenty years later they are still continuing.

In *Prayers That Are Answered* I share with you experiences— my own, my family's, friends'—some spectacular, some not

13

so spectacular. But each one unique, and each one has the same underlying theme: there is power in prayer.

This is not a definitive book on the subject of prayer; that's beyond my qualifications. Instead, my hope is that this book has a teaching role—a teaching role which I've entrusted to the Holy Spirit, asking that He use my own sometimes-faltering walk in faith to guide and help those who read it.

My personal discovery—begun 20 years ago in a beautiful world beyond this one—is that prayers are *really* answered.

1

PRAYER FOR A MATE

THE DRIVE ACROSS the causeway from the beach to the mainland was a quiet one. The tall, stately, royal palms flicked shadows against the pale red Florida sunset. Sunburned and tired tourists had lazily driven back to settle in their motels; the usual dinner traffic to the Kapok Tree Inn had long since disappeared.

The excitement of driving a new beige Thunderbird was muted by the lingering ache over my husband's death. How long had it been now? Two and a half years. Emotions were still intense. Memories pushed down on the top of my head; my breathing was smothered; inner emptiness crowded my rib cage. My two-year-old daughter April had fallen asleep on my lap, her little head of yellow, flaxen hair perspiring against the sunburned skin on my legs. Brenda, 14, leggy and colt-like, was dozing in the seat beside me, her head resting partly against the side window, partly on the seat cushion.

As I drove around Bayshore's scenic drive in Dunedin and then along highway 580, I struggled to calm my thoughts and feelings by recapturing the entire day. It was a Saturday; the year was 1968. The girls and I had taken our cabin cruiser, the *Betty Lynn*, for a short cruise into the bay. The boat had been built 10 years earlier for us by my grandfather's cousin, a retired boatbuilder. We had painted it jonquil yellow and

15

John, my husband, had named it for his two loves: me and
Brenda Lynn.

Launching the boat had been difficult for the two girls
and me, and our boat trips were becoming fewer and fewer.
Today's cruise into the gulf was a short one; the wind rose
and the coastal patrol ordered all small craft into shore.

April had silently stared at the water churning a deep green
by the side of the boat. Then she turned to me. "Mommy,
where is my name?"

I knew what she meant and tried to explain that her daddy
had died following open heart surgery four months before
she was born. Otherwise the boat might now be called, *Betty-
Lynn-April.*

After docking the boat, we had walked down the beach
to Baskin-Robbins in the pavilion for some ice cream. As
April ate her chocolate cone, she drew amused attention,
dressed in a lavender bikini, with sun glasses atop her head
like a movie star. Brenda had ordered pink bubble gum ice
cream, while I licked a mocha chocolate almond cone, smiling
at my two offspring on the outside but crying on the inside.
I felt lonely even in that happy crowd.

As we started out the door, April's eagle eyes spotted one
of those rocking horses on a post where you put a dime
in for a ride. Looking in my purse, I saw I had only bills
and one 50-cent piece and shook my head. I thought I had
made her understand the situation and we started toward the
door. Suddenly she reached out and grabbed a man by the
hand. "Mommie is broken," she said piteously. "She don't
have any dime for me to ride that horsey. Wouldja gimme
jist one dime?" I was humiliated. April, however, got the
dime.

Minutes later we were walking along a beach area, April
skipping ahead of Brenda and me. Stooping, her little ruffled
behind sticking out and upward, she touched the shoulder
of a bronzed, male figure covered with Coppertone oil,
sprawled out basking in the sun. "Wouldja be my daddy?"
she asked. "I got me no daddy."

We arrived at the scene just as the man's wife arose from her reclining position in the sun to demand an explanation. "Little Bit" had done it again.

The same scene had occurred the Sunday before as we were leaving church. April crawled up on the lap of a stern looking, elderly man, still seated in a nearby pew, and touching his rigid face, tenderly pleaded, "Wanna be my daddy?" It tore my heart.

As we drove into our driveway the fronds of the two palms on either side were like welcoming arms reaching out for us. Inside the house I served a glass of milk to the girls, heard their prayers, tucked them in bed with a good-night kiss and headed toward my bedroom and a bath. Resentment began to rise in me. How much longer would this loneliness continue? The cherry canopy bed seemed more desolate than usual. John's and my love nest for 14 years, it evoked bitter-sweet memories I wanted to put behind me.

Getting into the bathtub, two factions of my mind argued. People are right; I'll live for the girls and John's memory. My mind tells me this is right, but my body tells me that I'm only 34, and I crave physical love. The warm bath afforded small comfort as I buried my face in the wash cloth and cried, really cried, for the first time since my husband's death. The fear that I would never again feel strong arms around me, warm lips kissing me good-night, or know the comfort of engaging in pillow talk after a busy day, discussing tomorrow's plan, was unbearable.

I lost track of time sitting there, soaking in my bath while I bathed myself in self-pity. I heard the sound of my own muffled voice, moaning, praying "Oh God, my heavenly Father, in the name of Jesus Your Son, somewhere in this world find me a mate and send him to me."

Suddenly—I cannot tell you if it was an inner voice, or a wireless message from Heaven, or an angel whispering to me—but softly and plainly it registered: "At any moment in your life you may pray the prayer that will start the forces moving that will change your whole life."

Suddenly alert, I glanced at the clock. It was 10 P.M. I had been sitting there almost two hours. The water had grown cold, and I was shaking with a hard chill. The hope in that answer to my prayer gave me the energy to get out of the tub, towel off, and slip into my gown and bed.

Prayer was the key. Years before through prayer, I had invited Jesus into my life as Lord. He took the weight of sin and gave me loving forgiveness and purpose for living. If it was God's will, He would send me a mate.

Then another thought came. Before my prayer for a mate could be answered, I needed preparation. Men would not be attracted to me in a depressed state of self-pity. Men want women who are cheerful, who create a joyful, warm atmosphere of well-being into which they can enter. Oh, how much work God had to do on me!

Lying there in quiet prayer, the moonbeams that streamed across my bed reactivated my memory. I recaptured in keen detail the extraordinary experience of almost nine years before.

My appendix had ruptured, followed by peritonitis, many days in a coma, pneumonia, collapsed veins. And then my body functions had stopped. There was no heart beat and no breathing. A call had gone out from the hospital to my husband and parents, reporting my death. My dad had arrived first. He was met at the door of my hospital room by a nurse's aide attending my body which was covered with a sheet. All life support equipment had been removed.

Meanwhile, I was walking up a beautiful, green hill, following a radiant yellow light, a tall angelic presence by my side. We stopped outside a walled city. The gates dissolved, and I saw a Presence whose light flowed through me with cleansing, healing powers.

Standing there I saw shafts of light ascending from earth to heaven, powerful, direct rays beamed directly to the throne room where I felt the Great Light, the source of all energy and creative power. I *saw* prayers. I *heard* prayers. Then I observed one shaft of ascending prayer in the form of light and recognized the voice of my earthly father as he prayed a one-word prayer: "Jesus."

I turned back, feeling as though I was descending on an elevator. When the hospital reappeared, I felt myself drifting down to it and into room 336. Then sunbeams were streaming into the room across my bed. In the center of one sunbeam were ivory letters saying, "I am the resurrection and the life: he that believeth in Me, though he were dead, yet shall he live" (John 11:25).

When I reached up to touch these words of Jesus, the sheet fell off my face and life flowed into my fingers and down my arms into my body. I sat up before my weeping father. Two days later I went home.

There had been no fear of death after that experience, not even for my husband who passed away three and a half years later. Death was just changing locations. But was I beginning to fear the future of my life on earth if it had to be without a mate?

Sitting too long in chilled bath water seemed to delay sleep. As I tossed in bed, I recalled my paternal grandmother, Mom Perkins, saying, "There is an Adam for every Eve." God, in the book of Genesis, created Adam to commune with Him. Adam loved God but yearned for a natural person to share his garden Eden. God gave him Eve. I loved God and my children, and my need for a mate was not out of line.

Prayer, I realized, would become my lock and key. Prayer would lock me safely inside at night and would be my key to opening every day in the future.

I awakened early the next day, a Sunday. "What am I to do this morning?" I prayed. A change in ministers was taking place at our church, and I didn't want to go. The candidate preaching seemed too young and inexperienced.

But the inner voice was insistent. I was to go. Sighing, I awoke my daughters, and we drove to the cream-colored building with Spanish design which had been my church home for the past two years.

Standing to deliver his sermon, the young candidating pastor smiled at us. "I am Gary Chapin. If I become your pastor, I will seek to be a shepherd and a friend. I would not be announcing my sermon topics in advance but would spend much time each week in prayer that God show me your needs and give me the words on Sunday to meet them. At 10 P.M. last night God changed my sermon subject for this morning. The new title is: 'Self-Pity Is Sin.' If you have been bathing in self-pity, even for a legitimate reason, go home, and print these words—'Self-Pity Is Sin'—on a card and tack it up over your mirror or at your desk or on the refrigerator or by your telephone—some place where you will view it often."

Then he began to talk about Job. When Job began to whine, God spoke sharply. "Job, get up off the ashes of burned-out hope that you have been sitting on." Then a whirlwind came and blew away the ashes from under him. Having nothing to sit on, Job had to stand up. "Job's case was not hopeless," the preacher stated. "God never leads us to a dead end. It's impossible to look up into the face of God and say, 'Impossible.'

"Some of you in this audience need to stand up and get a clearer look at what's up and ahead, not down and back. Stand on the tiptoes of your faith and hope and prayer. When Job did this, God rewarded him with exactly twice of everything good that he had before his period of trial."

I sat there amazed. Could God love me so much to supernaturally move in this pastor's heart so that he would switch his sermon to a subject I desperately needed? For I had been sitting in a cold tub of despair at the very hour this pastor had changed his sermon.

"Quit feeling sorry for yourself, Betty; get up and get going," was the message I needed. If the flow of life passes by the person sunk in self-pity, then by an act of my will I would shake off my self-centeredness and move into the flow of life.

That very Sunday I volunteered for the church music program; in time I became the church organist and even sang for special occasions like weddings. This led to invitations to play the organ for funerals at Vinson Chapel in Tarpon Springs. Supplying music and personal comfort to grieving families helped me forget my own sorrow.

One morning I took April for her booster shot. The kindly doctor advised me to consider a second marriage. "If you don't find the right person—or should I say if that person doesn't find you—you should expose your daughters to good men: relatives, neighbors and church friends. Both of your girls need this exposure to develop normal and healthy attitudes toward men."

Driving home, I thought, *If he only knew.* I wanted to find the right man and so far had had two proposals: one from a 23-year-old "boy." I had thought he was coming to see Brenda until I learned that he thought by marrying me he would be exempt from the draft. The other was from Bob, twice my age and half my size. God love him; he hoped to win me through his money which he said would pay my bills and provide a maid to do my housework for me. I prayed that the Lord would lead him to someone who was both his size and his age. He found that person, and three months later they were happily married.

My dad and four brothers—Don, Jim, Marvin and Gary—spent generous time with the girls, supplying their need for male companionship and also tried to help answer my prayer by introducing me to eligible men. The first was Kurt, a male soloist who was trying out for a singing part in little theatre. He had a terrific voice, and I enjoyed playing the organ for him. This could be it. He looked like Uncle Jesse, my childhood hero.

After a few weeks of rehearsing with him, I could hardly recognize myself. I glowed. Riding the lawnmower, I sang loud and lustily. My voice could be heard above the roar of the motor. I even looked different in the mirror.

Kurt sent sentimental cards, a record, and a rose bud. He brought small gifts to the girls when he came to visit. It was good to feel cherished again. His attention and manners were almost too perfect.

One night we sat holding hands in the dark of the famous old Oslo Theatre in Sarasota. The seats were of plush mohair in dark red. The faint aroma of his "Canoe" aftershave was intoxicating—a pleasant forerunner of a new life for us both, I hoped. At intermission we were served citrus punch, made from local fruit, in a small garden. The two of us together in the setting of blossoming shrubs and blooming orchid trees made me feel positively heady. The drive home, soft music on the FM radio, the pleasant conversation and the light kiss good-night at the door kept me awake as I fantasized about what our life together would be like.

The next afternoon coming home from the grocery store, I glanced in the window of a lingerie shop. I went in, looked around and bought a black lace gown. This was my private secret. I slipped the package between two grocery sacks and upon arriving home dreamily hid it in the cedar chest in my bedroom.

If this was an illusion or a dream, don't wake me up. But there was always the lingering question, even in the theatre. Kurt possessed a mysterious, solemn melancholy that I could not interpret. And while romantically attentive, his touch was almost too light and deft. It haunted me. In my prayers I asked for an insight about him.

Several days later I received a phone call from a young woman. She would not give her name. "I am merely concerned for you and your two daughters. I dated Kurt," she explained. "Don't be impressed with his manners. He basically hates women. He is a wonderful dating partner but will never be a satisfying mating partner. He's gay."

I thanked her and hung up. I wanted to think that she had been jilted for me and was jealous.

Another concerned party sent me a clipping from a medical journal:

Not infrequently the man whom many women are inclined to regard as something special ("he's so attentive, always the perfect gentleman and he treats me like a queen") employs chivalrous behavior as a smoke screen to mask his real feelings and attitudes toward the opposite sex. As one psychologist has observed: "A good many of the so-called signs of respect for ladies are hangovers from a nonrespecting past and possibly are for some persons unconscious representations of a deep contempt for women."

After weeks of stubbornly closing my eyes, I opened them. My heart had played a trick on me. Kurt was strange in an unmasculine way. But why would he and others like him call themselves gay? They are basically *un*happy and depressed.

At the moment I was breaking off the relationship with Kurt, my friend, Beulah Brasker, living in Indiana, wrote me a short note to tell me that her heart had been broken. The young man she was engaged to marry had run off and married another woman. Beulah explained that she had wrapped her wedding gown in white tissue and put it in her hope chest. She had written the following poem in her disappointment and enclosed a copy in her letter to me.

Assurance

When the song in your heart is changed to a sigh,
    And your smile is replaced by a tear;
The sun has been hidden by a cloud in the sky
    And your peace has been robbed by a fear;

Your hopes which have builded a temple of dreams,
    Gold etching each detail with care,
Start crumbling to earth, and it seems
    That all is beyond repair;

'Tis good to remember that sweeter songs come
    When discordant notes have been quelled;
And the Great Master of music, is tuning your soul
    A sweeter song-story to tell.

A smile that is cheery dispels silent gloom,
    Lending brightness wherever you go;
But the Lord of the harvest doth seek precious grain
    That sowing in tears only grow.

So, smile when you're happy, and dream if you will,
  Be thankful when life's sun is bright;
But remember the dark cloud ushers in rain
  And daybreak follows the night.

Then I'll laugh, I will sing, when sad I will trust
  With a faith that is sure and sublime;
For He who delivered His Son for us all,
  Can master each problem of mine!

I closed my eyes, sitting with the letter and poem in my lap and prayed, "My heavenly Father, I thank you for the last line in Beulah's poem. You can master each problem of mine. The Bible says, 'my God shall supply *all* your needs.' Lord, I need a husband to make a living for us, to be a father to the girls and my 'partner for a purpose.' I do not feel You raised me from the dead to just struggle and get by. I need Your help now."

Confident that God would make something happen, I put a pink sunsuit on April and the two of us drove to the bank to cash in our last United Fund stock certificate. As I pulled into the bank parking lot, I saw smoke pouring from under the hood of the car. My feet were hot from flames now shooting from underneath.

In a panic I grabbed April, released her safety belt, and the two of us practically fell out of the door to safety. Since the fire department was only a block away, an engine arrived within minutes to quench the fire.

The fireman in charge was a tall, muscular man with tousled hair and a disarming grin. "The car's okay," he assured me. "Tell your husband it was faulty wiring. Not your fault."

When I explained that my husband was dead, he looked me over quickly, then had me fill out a report. Before he left he introduced himself as Phil. That night he called to ask if April and I were all right. Then he said he would like to come and visit me.

While having my car repaired, I inquired of the mechanic

concerning the fireman, Phil. He was not sure, but thought his wife was dead, since the children were usually with the grandmother.

Phil and I began going out. I was attracted by his rugged masculinity and his aggressive, take-charge manner. But he was reluctant to talk about himself. Finally he said he would write me a letter about himself.

He did, too—24 pages containing his full story in truthful detail. Phil was divorced and had eight children. His wife had been jealous of him. Once in a rage of temper he had bodily lifted the refrigerator from the kitchen and thrown it in the back yard. She had received a divorce on the grounds of "cruel and inhuman treatment." I was sorry for Phil, continued to talk with him on the phone, but knew anything beyond that was wrong.

I personally felt somewhat like the little boy who asked his daddy to fix a broken toy. When the father began to work on it, the boy kept sticking little fingers in the way, trying to tell him how to do it. Daddy finally rapped his boy's knuckles and set him on a chair nearby. "Son, you sit there quietly, trust me, and I'll fix it in half the time and twice as good." My knuckles had now been rapped twice by my Father.

When was God going to answer my prayers?

Months passed. Eligible men appeared, but most had to be warded off. I guess you should expect this when you are in your 30s, drive a Thunderbird and live in a house near Clearwater Beach with a guest cottage. What they didn't know was that the house was mortgaged and my trim figure was the result of a thin grocery budget.

A young minister, a widower, heard of me through a mutual friend. His name was Hal. He wrote, sent me the church bulletin, called on the phone, and the resonant quality of his voice convinced me that I would enjoy meeting him. Soon he was visiting me every Thursday.

I served him lunch on the patio, gave his little boys a collie puppy and felt his little guys needed me, since their mother had died from leukemia. Since he was a minister and I an organist, we both concluded that we would make a good team. I liked his wit and admired his pep, although I was too tall to walk comfortably beside him.

April was unimpressed. She prayed at her bedside one night shortly after one of his visits. Looking up toward the ceiling, she said, "Oh God, I want me a daddy for Christmas, but I don't want Hal. Him's too little. I want a big 'un."

Does God answer the superficial prayers of little children? Hal stopped visiting us soon after April's prayer. Seven weeks later I received his wedding announcement. I learned that the bride-to-be was younger, prettier, and could sing better than I. My pride was bruised.

Men—who needs them? I said to myself. I was tough, independent and could make it alone. I was no longer fearful at night since I had four collie dogs, the nine guns John left me and a father living eight miles away whom I could call on. More months passed.

One rainy night I put the girls to bed, kissed them goodnight and turned out the light just as the collies began to bark. Walking into my own room I undressed for a late bath. As I passed the open window "just as I am," I saw reflected in the mirror on the wall opposite the window, a face, two eyes peering at me with nose pressed against the glass. I almost fainted.

Then I looked closer. Relief flooded over me. It was "BB," my brother's shetland pony.

We had confined this little gelding with Princess, Brenda's mare who was in heat, in a fenced-in area behind the house. The barking of the dogs now alerted me to the fact that both pony and mare had probably broken loose.

I put a raincoat over my housecoat, ran outside to find that the collies had rounded up both animals near the fence gate. Just then help came. A car pulled into the driveway and a man I had known for years named Henry had been passing by on his way home when he saw the loose pony. I held the flashlight while he nailed the broken planks back in place and stretched barbed wire across the top of the fence.

Grateful, I thanked Henry and told him I wanted to pay him for his trouble and time. He touched my arm saying, "I've done you a favor; now I'll follow you into the bedroom where you can do a little favor for me."

Angry and hurt, I shut the door on him, catching part of Henry's hand. He removed it, and I closed and locked the door.

I cried for my John that night, for his boyish love, his respect and integrity. How I missed him! Then I propped myself up in bed and began reading the Bible. I stopped and prayed, "Lord, I no longer want to be like a reed shaken in the wind. Run a steel beam of faith up alongside my backbone that I may stand firm, trusting You to direct my life for the sake of my children." I read Psalm 4:4: "Commune with your own heart upon your bed, and be still." Psalm 31:1: "In Thee O Lord, do I put my trust; let me never be ashamed." Psalm 31:15: "My times are in Thy hand." Psalm 37:4–5: "Delight thyself also in the Lord; and He shall give thee the desires of thine heart. Commit thy way unto the Lord; trust also in Him; and He shall bring it to pass."

I reread Psalm 4:4, "Commune with your own heart upon your bed and be still." Relaxed, I leaned against the head of the bed with my eyes closed and fell asleep. I dreamed that I was sitting on a high, large rock, overlooking a pleasant meadow with a quiet brook winding through it, breezes blowing the long, light green fronds of a willow tree. I was viewing this pleasantry in a relaxed sitting position, my back and shoulders resting on a large open Bible, larger than I. It was open and parted, the front and back covers curved slightly to shelter and embrace my shoulders. In my dream, I turned slowly to read what I had rested against. In plain print on parchment paper with a snowflake-like finish I read Psalm 37:7: "Rest in the Lord, and wait patiently for Him."

When I awakened, I was resting against the head of my old cherry canopy bed, but I had the quiet, powerful assurance that I had communed with Almighty God, and He had talked to me. The desire to "gawk" for a husband was gone. I knew that if I would quit chasing rainbows that someday rainbows would chase me. I had been straining too hard to find God's will. When I learned to rest, His will would find me.

I looked down at my Bible, still open in my lap, and read on. Psalm 37:23: "The steps of a good man are ordered by the Lord: and he delighteth in His way."

Chills raced down my back. How right! God in His providence would order the steps of a good man toward me, not mine toward him, lending a quality of dignity to the arrangements.

Several more years passed as I battled discouragement, regularly pulling myself back to those words of the 37th Psalm. Then came a turning point in our lives. Brenda, now 17, decided she wanted to enroll at a college in Springfield, Missouri, where she would attend after high school. The girls and I drove there in January, and they had their first glimpse of snow. After Brenda was enrolled, we began motoring through the old, historic section of town when suddenly I stopped the car to stare at a lovely Victorian jewel of a house. It was thirsty for paint and badly in need of repair but had a mysterious looking tower in the front. There were three stories, porches all around and a porch swing sitting in the shrubs. Old oak and walnut trees surrounded the house. All my childhood dreams of living in a picture-book house with fireplaces and winding staircases surfaced.

From the house next door came a man who hammered a sign into the ground: FOR SALE BY OWNER. My steps were sure as I walked up to the man. "Sir, please don't display that sign. I would like to buy this house. May we see the inside and talk with you about the details?" He agreed.

Inside we found it to be a happy house, unlike the dark gloomy Victorian homes I had visited. It was done in pastels and white with an airy, pleasant atmosphere. It had a circular stairway and two fireplaces. One had an Italian marble hearth and mantle. I could picture Brenda bringing homesick college students here; we would fill all 12 rooms with their music and laughter.

When the owner agreed to accept a binder of $1,000 which would hold the house for 30 days, the girls and I returned to Florida to sell our house there. One week before the balance was due on the Springfield house, the Florida home sold.

It seemed a wild and impulsive step, but to the three of us it was so right. We needed a change. We wanted to be together. The house was such a delight and challenge. Right at that moment we submitted it all to the Lord and asked Him to help us work out the details—if He approved.

The first Sunday night after we arrived back in Springfield to take over our new home, we went to a large, nearby church. It was a refreshing change from the small one we had attended for the past nine years which had been made up mostly of retired people. Looking around, Brenda became excited to see so many high school and college students. It all seemed so right.

In late spring, the educational director of our church persuaded me to teach a class for Vacation Bible School planned for early summer. At the very first session of this class I noticed a girl on the fourth row who had the largest, saddest eyes I had ever seen. They were pale green with a "wounded dove" expression far too mature for her 14 years.

Later as punch and doughnuts were being served, this girl brought her refreshments to me, introduced herself as Connie, and asked, "May I sit with you?" Then out poured her story. Her mother had recently died of cancer. Her father was overseas raising funds for a Christian publishing house. "When he comes home, I'd love to introduce you to him," she said shyly. "He's lonely. I never thought I'd want another mother, but you're the first woman I've met that I would like to be my mother."

Her gentle frankness touched my heart. I shared with her my sorrows: a husband dead from open heart surgery and my mother also gone from cancer. I told her, yes, it would be nice to meet her daddy sometime.

April and I were driving home from a Wednesday night church service weeks later when she asked, "Mommie, can I have toast with butter and sprinkle tonight?" Sprinkle was what we called cinnamon mixed with sugar. Remembering that we had used the last slice of bread for sandwiches, I pulled into a grocery store at the small shopping center, quickly picked up a loaf of bread and was standing with April in the express lane of the check-out counter. April was having a conversation with a man in line behind us. He was so attentive to her that I could tell he loved children.

Curious, I turned around and looked into a pair of warm, deep blue eyes. He was a tall, sturdily-built man wearing a London Fog raincoat. His complexion was tanned; the voice was deeply resonant.

When the man at the cash register called "58 cents" for my loaf of bread, I opened my coin purse. It was empty! Yet that morning I had started out with a five, two one-dollar bills and some change. I had seen the money in my purse at church. Had April done it again? Once before while I played the organ she had opened my purse and put my last 20 dollar bill in the offering plate. Embarrassed, I stood there staring at my empty purse.

"May I help out?" It was the deep-voiced man behind us.

"Oh no, I can't let you do that," I said awkwardly. I turned to the clerk, "I'll go home and get the money and return for the bread later."

But the man behind me insisted, the transaction was made, the sale rung up. I squeezed out a limp, "Thank you," took April's little hand and hurried out the door and into the car. The whole episode reeked of a contrived, cheap manipulation. I felt humiliated and hoped I would never encounter my benefactor again.

In the car I turned to April. "Did you put Mommie's money in the offering tonight?"

"No, Mommie, I put it in my purse in church to play with and keep me quiet during the singing."

Sure enough, there in her little shoulder bag was $7.26.

As I drove slowly out of the parking lot, I noticed a girl with large, sad, green eyes coming out of the Dairy Queen, licking an ice cream cone. Her face was familiar. Of course: she was Connie, the girl in Vacation Bible School whose mother had died and who wanted me to meet her father.

Then she climbed into a green Chevrolet Vega where a man was sitting behind the wheel. Her father, no doubt. I looked closer. A tall, sturdily-built man in a London Fog raincoat.

2

THE ANSWER

SUNDAY MORNING Brenda was ready for church early, which was unusual. Going to church had suddenly become interesting to her with the scores of young people in her youth group. But I was far from eager. The prospect of meeting Connie and her father embarrassed me. The church was large, I thought with relief. Perhaps I could be lost in the crowd. Then too, Connie's father traveled so much he might not even be there.

April, Brenda and I found three seats on the side of the nearly full sanctuary. The song service began, and I heard a deep, male voice singing lustily four or five rows behind us. I did not have to look; I knew that voice from the previous Wednesday night at the grocery store.

All through the sermon I felt eyes watching me. Usually in church I forgot everything else, but this morning I could not. When the congregation stood for the prayer of benediction, I whispered to Brenda, "Let's slip out the exit door to avoid the crowd. I left a roast in the oven. It might dry out." She grimaced, wanting to talk to young people, then nodded. We made our escape. Or did we?

We were finishing our dessert about an hour later when the phone rang. "This is Carl Malz. My daughter Connie has talked about you so much that I thought I would call and thank you for your kindness to her. I wanted to talk to you in church today, but you left before I could reach you."

"We had to hurry home," I said somewhat breathlessly. *Why is my heart racing?*

"I watched you this morning in church," he continued. "You didn't know it (Oh, didn't I?), but we sat several rows behind you. I noticed how attentive you were with your children. That impressed me. You'd be surprised how few mothers want their children with them."

"April, Brenda and I are very close," I said. The coolness in my voice didn't deter him. He chatted on about parents and children for a while. Then he shifted direction.

"Could the five of us get together some evening? Perhaps for dinner? Connie wants to know Brenda better."

He came on too strong, too soon. I put him off, made an excuse; then annoyed with myself, I suggested he call back later.

After hanging up the phone, I was churning inside. What was wrong with me? A few years ago I had been so lonely that I sat in my bath fantasizing about men until the water became frigid. Now an eligible widower was starting to pursue me, and I was running away from him. It was baffling.

The next time Carl called he talked so long my left ear was burning, my left elbow aching and almost numb. He told me about the circumstances which led him to Springfield, Missouri, instead of to London, England. He talked about his wife, Wanda, and her death.

He elaborated on his concern for Connie, who had been born in India, educated in Egypt in a French Catholic boarding school and was now becoming quiet and passive with approaching puberty and adolescence. Did I have any suggestions to help her? I learned that he had been the president of Southern Asia College, had established two theological seminaries overseas and was now writing several college courses. His present job was vice president of the International Correspondence Institute (ICI) for which he had to make overseas trips to England, Switzerland and Belgium.

I learned that he had two married children: son, Carl David and Diane Malz; daughter, Carol and Jack Acuff.

Before the phone conversation ended, I mentioned that the following Thursday, November 6, was my birthday. We made plans for the five of us to celebrate at a little French restaurant in Branson, Missouri.

Connie and Brenda put April between them in the back seat of Carl's Vega and entertained her all the 40 miles to Branson. Soft music on the FM radio played, "We've Only Just Begun." I avoided Carl's eyes when the song title registered and dug in my mental heels. I had been disappointed by men too many times the past six years and was determined to move with utmost caution.

The restaurant was quaint with red linen tablecloths; we had a table near a window with a view. The waitress thought we were a family and treated us as such. As we talked I studied Carl. He was not handsome, yet his nose and facial bones were strong and masculine. He had dark hair, his eyes were clear and direct, his voice deep. Assertiveness was his most prominent quality, and I wasn't sure I liked it at all.

At one point he cautioned that we should be careful not to start gossip. That annoyed me. He worried too much about what people thought. I wanted someone carefree and easy-going like John had been.

This birthday celebration was a nice gesture, but suddenly I was anxious to be back in the security of my own house where I could be myself and say what I pleased. The alone-ness of my life had its pluses after all. I felt my independence being threatened, and this was only our first date.

When we were finished eating, the older girls took April to the ladies' room. Carl quickly moved the candle a little distance away and leaned close. Putting an arm on my chair, he said, "It is good to feel we are a family. I think I'm falling in love with you, Betty. I began to feel strongly attracted to you in the grocery when you were so embarrassed. At your worst you are better than any woman I know at her best. You laugh a lot. Connie and I need that. I like your girls, the way they enjoy animals and pets, the way you all enjoy simple things. Connie has never had a chance to live that way. She's spent most of her life in apartment buildings in strange, foreign cities. She dreads the thought that we might have to move to Brussels. I feel God has brought us together . . ."

The girls returned, and I was relieved. Carl's directness made me dizzy, confused. I was in full retreat from his obvious and serious intentions.

"But you hardly know me," I said to him later when we were alone again for a few moments. "And I certainly don't know you."

"I know more about you than you think," he said with assurance.

"Well, I sure don't feel the way you do," I said firmly.

Carl left town shortly thereafter on a business trip. I thought I had thoroughly dampened his ardor until the cards started coming: pretty cards, silly cards, serious cards and post cards. All of them were addressed to "Eve" from "Adam" with no return address. His whimsical use of these names startled me. What was my grandmother's favorite expression? "There's an Adam for every Eve."

Two days before Christmas he returned and called to see when we could get together. "My daughter, Carol, and her husband, Jack, are here for the holiday. They would like to meet you," he said.

I invited them over for dessert that evening. Then I prepared a date roll made from an Old English recipe that some of my ancestors had brought from England; I found some hand-dipped chocolates which Brenda had made. When the Malzes arrived I lit candles on either side of a crystal punch bowl and we gathered in the living room waiting for the punch to chill. Right away I liked Carol and Jack. While we chatted I heard a clattering in the dining room. Everyone jumped up, and we all rushed to see if something had broken or fallen. We found April kneeling on a chair. On her head was Papaw Perkins' old hunting hat with the bullet hole through the top. She was leaning over the punch bowl drinking from the ladle.

It was a hilarious sight. I stole a look at Carl. My irrepressible girls might quickly turn him off as a suitor. But Carl was laughing too.

After refreshments Carl brought in beautifully wrapped gifts for us all. As the girls unwrapped theirs and thanked him, I was warmed with affection at his generosity. I knew it was a sacrifice for him. His economic situation was as bad as ours—maybe worse. His wife had gone through a long illness, and missionaries live a sacrificial life.

In an elaborate ceremony he presented me with a miniature grandfather clock to set on the mantle. "Girls, when you hear it chime, it is saying, 'I love your mother.' "

I was overwhelmed at these words in front of everyone. What transparent honesty and feelings! And such a contrast to the men I had encountered during the past years.

The last package I opened was a red, calfskin, carry-on bag with a shoulder strap. "Who knows what kind of traveling you may be doing in the future?" he said with a confident smile.

As we sat in the living room getting acquainted, April slid onto the couch, then crawled up on Carl's lap, putting her arm around his neck. Grinning, she looked at me and said, "He's a big 'un, Mommie!"

I pretended not to hear, but I couldn't avoid stealing a glance at Brenda who was looking at me with a knowing smile. She too recalled April's prayer several years before—"for a daddy, and please Lord, a big 'un."

After they left and the girls were asleep, I tried to ponder the situation rationally. There were moments when Carl was very dear and I wanted to be in his arms. Then came moments when I was glad when he was out of town and I was free again. I loved his attitude toward the girls, and his generosity overwhelmed me. Yet he was eight serious years older than

I. He was too aggressive, possibly due to his active life as an endurance swimmer, jogger and avid handball player.

During my prayer time the next few days, I seemed to hear the words, "Find out what others think of Carl." The first opportunity came through an old friend, Roy Wead, president of Trinity College in Ellendale, North Dakota. He and his wife, Rosa Mae, had given me a white Bible after my high school graduation which I carried in my wedding when I was married to John. When Dr. Wead came to visit one day I pulled out a brochure containing Carl's picture from my purse and asked him, "Do you know this man?"

There was instant recognition: "I've known Carl all his life. He's a prince! Dedicated to his work, devoted to God and his family. Sad about his wife, Wanda. She died of cancer. Why do you ask?"

"He wants to marry me."

Dr. Wead was thoughtful. "I wouldn't have thought of putting two opposites like you together, but why not? You couldn't do better."

I told him that Carl would probably have to move overseas which I wasn't sure would be right for Brenda and April.

"That's interesting. I'm here on faculty business to hire a man who can serve the college as a professor of foreign missions and be a campus pastor. Carl is experienced in both fields. He could train and recruit young missionaries. If you do decide to get married, have Carl come and talk to me."

A bit dazed by this turn of events, I went to see a friend who had already gone through what I would experience if I married Carl and went overseas with him to set up our new home. She advised against it. "The adjustment to a foreign culture and new parents is too much for young children. It involves more than it appears to. Don't do it. If you get married, stay in the states until the girls adjust to Carl."

Next on my agenda was my father. I learned that he had known Carl some years before. Carl had spoken in my father's church when he, with his wife and three children, was home on furlough from India. I seldom ask people for advice, but I asked my Dad, too, for his. He gave it. "Betty, decide with your head, not with your emotions."

That evening when April had been tucked into bed, I kept Brenda up and talked confidentially with her. "Mother," she said, "I can relate to and respect an intelligent man like Carl. Frankly, if you turn him down, I'll be disappointed."

The following night when I was almost asleep, the phone rang. I knew who it was before I picked up the receiver. After a warm, chatty description of his travels through the East, he took me back with his directness. "Betty, I believe we are meant for each other. I'm not a boy. I play for keeps. I am not interested in dating—only marrying. If your answer is no, tell me so. If you're not sure, let's pray about it and keep seeing each other. I don't want to play games, so I'll tell you frankly that if you're still uncertain, I want to visit a nurse living here. She served as a medical missionary with us in India. She has never married and has returned here for further training in a veterans' hospital."

The man's openness was startling and also appealing. "Please go see her, Carl," I urged. "This may be the deciding factor. With her background and training she may be what you need rather than me."

When I hung up, I sat quietly in the dark of the living room of our old Victorian house. A few dying embers in the fireplace gave a small amount of illumination, and the street light filtered through the tree branches casting shadows across the old-fashioned porch and through the oval, leaded glass of the door. In many ways this was the house of my childhood dreams, though it was not quite redecorated yet. The place was growing on me; I was putting down roots. I was tired of moving about. While I realized that a house is not a home without the love of a husband, the element of acceleration in Carl's personality frightened me. Carl's creed seemed to be: He who hesitates is lost! Gamble . . . risk it . . . leap at life . . . anything worth doing is worth doing fast!

My English family did things slowly, deliberately. I had always believed in taking it easy. "All good things come to those who wait." Carl decided things so hastily I wondered if he had some special kind of rapport with God in receiving guidance. Or could it be a flaw in his nature that would fragment our home and bring discomfort in marriage? I prayed, "Lord, urge Carl to go and visit his nurse friend. If she is the right one for him, then that will relieve me of the responsibility of making this decision. I am not missionary material. She's had years of experience in that sort of life. I've had none."

I groped through the next day, finding it hard to concentrate. One minute courage would rise, and I'd tell myself, "I'll take the chance. I'll say yes." The next minute, I would reason, "I'm not a good mover. If he went overseas, that would be exciting but very difficult. If he took a job with Dr. Wead, we would have to move to North Dakota. Where exactly is North Dakota?"

Finally I got out a map and found it. Then I compared its location to my last home in Florida. It was a leap from the southernmost state almost to the northernmost. I had always prided myself in being flexible, but this was ridiculous!

That evening the boys at the fraternity house nearby were initiating new house members. Part of their ritual was carrying a canoe over their heads, marching up the street singing loudly. The noise drove Missy, our collie, to excited barking. When the college boys began shooting firecrackers, fireworks and rockets, it was too much for Missy. She took off. We searched until dark, up and down streets, knocking on the doors of friends. Then we called the Society for the Prevention of Cruelty to Animals and alerted them to watch for her. The police were also alerted. The girls and I went to bed with heavy hearts.

In the morning Missy had not returned. Sadly I went to the mail box, hoping for some word. There was one plain, white envelope with no return address. Inside I read:

                            Adam
                    Oh, God
                    Of all completeness
                    In all creation
                    I, alone, am incomplete.

                    See the man
                    That Thou has formed
                    In Thy perfection?
                    With one exception . . .

                    Alone
                    I found within
                    A haunting cry
                    That echoed through
                    The empty chambers of my heart.

                    Until . . .
                    From slumber You imposed,
                    I rose,
                    To find another at my side.
                    We touched,
                    The echoes died.

Another anonymous note from Carl. I suddenly realized that here was not an impetuous rush act. This rawboned, rugged man was pursuing the woman he loved with ardor and determination. He intended to build a steady and meaningful life for the girls and for me. Always before I had thought a man who wrote poetry to be effeminate. No more. This masculine creature was six foot three inches tall, weighed 220 pounds and had a tender overflowing heart.

A new awareness stabbed me. In His way, God was providing a strong man to satisfy my physical needs, a man with a keen mind to stimulate my intellect and a Christian faith that would bind us together. We could pray together. The Bible says, "One will chase a thousand, but *two* can put ten thousand to flight." Two of God's children are 10 times as effective as one. What I was experiencing was not a crush but the beginnings of genuine love.

As I read the poem a second time I had a sudden qualm. I had urged Carl to visit the nurse. Was the poem a kind way to let me know that Adam had found his true Eve? *Oh God, is it too late for me?* The nurse had never been married and perhaps had waited anxiously for a chance like this, possibly for years. It would be easier for Carl too. She had no children; he would not have to adjust to stepchildren.

The glow of my new love for Carl was replaced by a sick apprehension. I had lost Carl. Why had I been so slow to realize his superior qualities? Why had I so glibly pushed him into the arms of that nurse?

A feeling of loss began to overwhelm me. First it was Missy. If we ever saw our collie again, it would be a miracle. Now Carl was gone.

The phone rang and I leaped for it. It was Carl. "Don't talk, just listen," he began. "I could not visit the nurse. I came home after work last night and started to call her. Then suddenly I knew I shouldn't do it. You are right for me and for Connie. Everyone agrees but you. Even your dog is trying to tell you something."

"Have you seen Missy?" I asked, astonished.

"Yes, At five this morning I heard a cry at the back of the house, near my study window. I looked out, and when I didn't see anything, I opened the door. There stood a collie dog. Betty, I'm sure it is yours. I don't know how she found our house. She couldn't have known where we live, and she'd have to face miles of traffic to get here. She is in Connie's bedroom now. The pads on her paws are red and sore, and one of them is bleeding a little. She must have walked and paced all night. I'll bring her to you."

Stunned, overwhelmed, I went upstairs and awakened the girls, put on a fresh pot of coffee and brushed my hair. In a short time, Carl, Connie and Missy were at the dining room door. The girls went wild, pounding Connie on the back, patting the dog, kissing her cold nose, hugging Carl.

I ran up to him and whispered in his ear, "Yes, yes, yes." Up to this point I had disliked his too-solemn, too-serious

manner. It had vanished. That moment he came alive, hilari-
ously whooped and swung me around like a lariat.

For the remainder of the morning we all began making
wedding plans.

Later that evening Carl stopped by on his way out of town.
He did not come in, just to the door. "Close your eyes,"
he said. He took my hand and slipped a ring onto my left
ring finger. It was a plain, gold band with a crest on top
which looked somewhat like the cross of Jesus Christ. Carl
explained that it was from Egypt and called "a key to life"
ring. For centuries Egyptians had painted and carved this
crest on the tombs of their dead. Though they rejected the
God of Moses, the Egyptians chose for a symbol a replica
of the cross on which Christ would die. How fascinating that
they would then call it a "key to life" symbol, even before
Jesus said that He was the only Key to the next life.

It was also a unique engagement ring for me since I had
tasted death and then returned to tell others about it.

Carl asked me to choose the date. Since I had always wanted
to be a June bride and since Carl was marrying three of us
and since the Triune Godhead had been responsible for
bringing us together in such a divine and miraculous way,
I chose June 3. Carl seemed somewhat startled by my decision, pondered it a moment, then nodded.

The wedding was an occasion of quiet beauty. At the foot
of the winding stairway of our Victorian house we set up a
white archway. On each side we placed a palm, a potted
fern, and a candelabra holding three candles. I made dresses
of soft-pink shell knit for Brenda, Connie and April.

My dress was a full-length gown, three tiers of white Nat-
chez lace. My bouquet was simple: seven blue daisies nestled
in babies' breath, bordered with one sprig of fern, tied to
the small white Bible that Roy and Rosa Mae Wead gave
me for high school graduation, the same Bible I had carried
when John and I were married.

My father flew in to perform the ceremony. Brenda stood
by me; Connie was beside her daddy, and April stood in

the center between Carl and me. Carol and Jack, and a writer friend, Ruth Lyon, looked on. My cup would have overflowed if only my mother could have been alive to be there. Her prayers had sustained me during the first months of my widowhood.

When my father asked Carl the question, the "I do" came through with robust enthusiasm. Then, turning to me, Daddy repeated the question.

I took both of Carl's hands in mine, and looking into the pale blue eyes of the man to whom I was entrusting my future and the future of my children, I repeated from memory verses 1 and 17 of chapter one of the Book of Ruth: "Entreat me not to leave thee, or to return from following after thee: for whither thou goest I will go; and where thou lodgest, I will lodge: thy people shall be my people, and thy God, my God: Where thou diest, will I die, and there will I be buried: the Lord do so to me, and more also, if aught but death part thee and me."

Carl's face let me know how meaningful these words were to him. For me it was more than a spiritual gesture; it represented a heart attitude of faith in the future, for at that point I did not know if we would be moving to London, Brussels, or North Dakota.

During our wedding supper the Malz side of the family could keep the secret no longer. When I had chosen the wedding date, June 3, I had no way of knowing that this was also Carl's and Wanda's wedding date and also the wedding date of Carl's mother and father.

Carl's humorous courtship communications as "Adam" led to the choice of our honeymoon site, Eden's Isle, located in the heart of the Ozark Mountains in Arkansas. The lodge was rustic and surrounded by wooded lakes. The honeymoon suite had separate lavatories, above which were two little plaques, one for "Adam" and the other for "Eve." On the coffee table were huge, red, polished apples. The bath mat, the soap, the shower curtains, everything had apples on them, and a small bronze plate imbedded in the mantle of the old stone fireplace said: "Adam and Eve . . . for your pleasure during your stay at Eden's Isle."

When we began to count our blessings and ponder over the miraculous, mysterious way we met, I asked Carl a question that had been bothering me for months. "Since the Bible clearly says to ask what you will and it *shall* be granted, why did it take six long years for God to answer?"

As we talked, it became obvious that God had used circumstances to bring Carl and me together. In His wisdom and knowledge of the future, God saw that the day would come when we needed each other—not just Betty needing the right man in her life, but Carl and Betty needing each other. And at the appointed time He'd used our mutual need and still allowed us our individuality as the relationship struggled for recognition and stability. Carl had his God-given persistence; I had to learn to recognize God's signals. As a result, we were brought together in love.

"You know," I told my new husband, "I kept looking at what I thought was the immensity of the problem. But when God answered my prayer, He did so in such a small incident— an empty pocketbook."

The first Sunday morning after our honeymoon, Carl, Connie, Brenda, April and I were sitting together in church— as a family. It was like a dream come true. The dreamlike situation would continue for a while, but then real life would bring many serious new areas that demanded prayer.

3

FAMILY PRAYER

CARL AND I had laughed when an 80-year-old friend wrote us: "If your marriage works, it will be a miracle. Betty is a Scorpio and Carl a Gemini. A Scorpio never marries a Gemini."

As Christians we know we should not look to the horoscope for guidance but to Jesus Christ. In his prayer at our wedding my father said, "Lord, be their ever-present help in time of need. Where there is a lack, You make up the difference."

After our honeymoon trip Carl and Connie moved out of their apartment into the Victorian house and the problems involved in bringing together two broken families began. One night I awakened suddenly in the darkness of our bedroom. Carl was not beside me. Then I heard a strange sawing, crunching noise. Paralyzing thoughts raced through my mind. Someone was trying to saw the lock off on the kitchen door. Carl must have heard it before I awakened and had gone to apprehend the burglar.

Terrified, I jumped out of bed and crept to my bureau. Reaching to the bottom of my "undie" drawer I drew out the little Italina Beretta six-shooter I had always kept in my bedroom for protection. Then I moved stealthily down the steps, convinced that my husband was in trouble and needed me.

Slowly I pushed open the swinging door to the kitchen.

My gun was cocked, my hand was shaking, but I was ready to defend our home.

"Betty!!!" It was Carl. We both stood there paralyzed. I had come close to shooting my new husband!

Carl and I held each other for several moments; then came the questioning. "It's 3:20 in the morning. Why are you up so early?"

"I get hungry. My day has begun at 4 A.M. with grape nuts almost every morning of my life," he said calmly.

"I thought a burglar was sawing off the lock. Instead, it's you crunching cereal. What other strange habits do you have?"

"Nothing that you can't adjust to," he said cooly.

I decided to tease him a bit. "Honey, look in the mirror at your hair. You could play 'Alfalfa' in the Little Rascals cartoons."

"When I married you," he replied, "I didn't expect a combination of Carol Burnett and Phyllis Diller. At 4 A.M., however, your comedy is a bit flat."

I turned and started to leave the kitchen. He took one step toward me and that was all I needed. I turned back, we embraced, then I promised to check my impulsive tongue and he promised to be more quiet when he got up so early in the morning. We both laughed uneasily at the problems we knew lay ahead. When two people get married they have only two adjustments to make—each to the other. When a family of five people like us get married, that requires 20 adjustments: five people in their new roles adjusting to four others.

But our promises were short-lived. The verbal warfare flared time after time. Once as we drove home from a party at friends' I felt a cloud hanging over us. When we were in the house, I followed Carl into the darkened living room where we immediately sat at opposite ends of the sofa.

"Well, Betty, you did it again," he began. "You embarrassed me with your laughing and clowning. Must I always play straight man for your jokes?"

"Well!" I snapped back at him, "You seem to always bring out the *worst* in me!"

"True," he thundered, "but something cannot come *out* that is not already *in.*"

I suddenly felt like I was watching one of the afternoon soap operas on television. "Can this marriage be saved?" In the exchange that followed I let Carl know that he was too serious, too critical, too much a perfectionist—and wasn't God.

It was as though Carl had been saving green stamps and had a whole book of them to cash in. "John may have told you that you run a perfect household, but I disagree. For example—that collie breathes on my elbow when I get in bed with you. I step on the cat every time I go to the fireplace. You and your girls run around in faded denims and bare feet. Betty, you're a 'woodsy.'"

At that moment Connie, his daughter, tripped down the stairs, heard the last sentence and walked over to us. She bent down, kissed me on the cheek, quietly looked up at her dad and said, "I love this 'woodsy.' Life had gotten too serious for us, Daddy. She's teaching us to laugh again."

Just as quietly as she entered, Connie went back up the stairs, leaving us both a bit stunned.

"We're going to make it," Carl said firmly. We sat together on the couch, still in the dark, my head on his shoulder, and agreed that there was much at stake. We needed to laugh and pray more. Then we discussed how different we were, this time in fun.

Carl enjoys spending money; I am thrifty. He was born in the city of Cleveland; I grew up in the country. He likes to go out; I like to stay in. He is a mover; I'm a stayer. He's educated far beyond average; I majored in kids and collies. He likes animals to stay outside; I like a dog and cat indoors. He drinks his coffee bubbling hot, with cream and sugar; I like mine warm and black. He eats dark bread and I like white. He gulps his breakfast, standing up at the kitchen sink to save time; I like a leisurely breakfast during

which I can sip coffee and juice slowly, even outside under
the wisteria vine. He sleeps with three blankets; I like only
one. He likes the windows down; I like them up. He's solemn;
I laugh too much. He likes large-curd cottage cheese; I like
small-curd. Carl drives slowly; I drive fast. He's German and
I'm English. He gets four to five hours sleep a night; I need
nine. He gets up at 4:00 A.M.; I prefer the alarm to ring at
7:00 A.M. He likes the slow refrain; I like fast music. Carl
tingles at tragedy in drama; I prefer comedy.

We concluded that we both did like black licorice, we loved
children, we knew how to pray and pray we would—pray
we must.

But inside I was frightened. The contrast between us was
so sharp. The problems of bringing together two broken
families were greater than I had realized. Had we married
too quickly? I feared that if the tensions between us were
transmitted to the children, our home could become a battle-
ground of arguments and flare-ups.

Carl and I decided to pray together every day. This was
a good start. I also sought time to pray alone to try and
deal with the qualities in me which I knew were not pleasing
to Carl and I sensed were not pleasing to God either.

Four weeks after our marriage Carl accepted President
Wead's offer of a teaching-pastoral post at Trinity College
in Ellendale, North Dakota. In the days that followed we
sold the Victorian house, packed, had a farewell party with
the people of Carl's former organization—International Correspondence Institute—and then headed north.

When we arrived in Ellendale, Carl began teaching at the
college while I began making a home out of the eight-room
house we bought on the outskirts of this town of 12,000
people. It too was a lovely home: old Spanish design, 38
acres with a pond and 300 pine trees. We quickly named it
"Whispering Pines." Brenda enrolled at Jamestown College
in Jamestown, North Dakota, 60 miles to the north; Connie
was a junior in high school, and April loved first grade.

Soon our two older girls would be moving out on their own. Within two years of our arrival in North Dakota, Brenda married a young man she met in college, Bud Smart, and they moved to Columbia, Missouri, where Bud could complete his studies. One year later Connie and Steve Bobzien— a young man from Ellendale who was enrolled in college at Wahpeton, North Dakota, at the time—would be married.

Meanwhile, about a year after moving to Ellendale, April balked at entering the second grade. The first day we took her. The second day we virtually pushed her out the door to meet the school bus. The third day she cried while walking down the driveway toward the bus, then turned and ran back up to the house when the bus arrived.

On the fourth day I went with April to the door of the elementary school. She threw herself down on the lawn in front of the school, crying and begging me not to make her go inside. Several passersby stopped, wondering, I'm sure, if I were abusing the child. After April finally disappeared into her classroom, I sobbed all the way home.

Our prayers did not seem to touch the situation. School seemed to terrify April, and she went only under great pressure and persuasion. Often I let her stay home because I lacked the stamina and strength to force her to go.

What made it even more embarrassing was that I was writing a folksy column for the local newspaper, *The Leader*. It was called "Betty's Bits" and was filled with kernels of news, observations and humor. Townspeople who expected a columnist to have accumulated a large store of wisdom must have been surprised at my helplessness in getting my troubled child into the front door of the school.

I wanted to run and hide. Run I did—into my clothes closet where I shut the door and, according to scripture, prayed for help.

The guidance came when I was reminded that God never promised us a smooth life, that I could have all of God I wanted if I let Him have all of me that He wanted. It seemed

to me that God was closing doors all *about* me, but He had
not shut the door *above* me.

When I admitted to God that my pride was getting in the
way and that I didn't know all the answers, the door opened
for Carl, April and me to go to a fine children's psychiatrist,
Dr. Awad Ismir, in nearby Jamestown. After a series of con-
sultations, he took Carl and me into a private room away
from April to give us his findings. I have summarized them
here:

A thorough physical examination indicates no physical problems.
Since April is an "A" student, she does not have a learning problem.
No teacher or principal has harassed or abused her. By questioning,
I find that April loves her stepfather almost as much as her natural
mother. The source of her problem is quarreling, criticism, unrest,
tension and pressure in the conflict between you, her parents. True,
you don't hit each other or even scream and shout at each other.
You shoot "velvet arrows" at each other. This child is extremely
intelligent and very sensitive. She feels she cannot go to school
because she must stay home to keep you, her parents, from hurting
each other. Through experiment with tiny newborn babies, we have
learned that trouble and/or a negative atmosphere in the home
registers with them even when they are sleeping in the next room
and don't even hear the conflict.

Carl, you should quit sweating the small stuff. Don't be so techni-
cal. So what if there is dust on the curio cabinet. If Betty is doing
all these creative, worthwhile things you say she is, she does not
have time to dust the curio cabinet.

Betty, don't try to make Carl a carbon copy of yourself or someone you wish you had married. If you would succeed at making
a chameleon of him, you'd *lose!* Relax and let the five members
of your family relax.

He hit us between the eyes. We were mortified! Here we
were two Christian parents whose quarreling was destroying
our home.

Every morning after that we sat down with the girls while
Carl read a comforting verse of scripture. Then he would
say, "Okay, Mommie, let's made a kid sandwich." We would

put April in the middle, with one of us on either side. Each of us would hug her while Carl prayed: "Oh Lord, be with April on the bus and on the playground. Give her a happy day in the classroom, and send her home safely to us this evening. We love You, God. We love April and we love each other. Amen."

The change did not come immediately but weeks later. One morning I saw April skipping down the driveway, green lunchbox in her hand. The collie dogs wagged their tails as she waved good-by, blew us a kiss and hopped on the big orange monster that swallows her up each morning to take her to the elementary school.

It has been painful to my pride to tell this story. In my prayer time, however, I knew He was urging me to be more honest and open about my weaknesses. He showed me that the yardstick for revealing a personal experience is whether it could help someone else and glorify Him. I was first taught to pray at two; I was learning to pray at 42. Whenever I feel my days are too full to pray, I read this verse:

> I woke up early this morning
> And paused before entering the day.
> I had so much to accomplish,
> That I *had* to take time to pray.

The bumps and upsets continued in our married life, but Carl and I had a more solid base now to deal with them through our prayers together. When he would call from work upset about something, we would pray about it over the phone. Since Carl and I were such opposites, we knew we had to seek the humor in difficult situations whenever possible. One day we visualized Wanda and John, our former mates, sitting up there in the heavenly balcony praying for us to get our act together and laughing at our clumsy efforts to adjust.

As our prayer life grew, we bought two file boxes, marked one "Prayer Requests" and the other, "Prayers Answered."

On separate three-by-five cards we listed our prayer needs. When an answer came, as it did with April's school problem, we wrote out the answer and how it came about and transferred the card to the "Prayers Answered" box. But we were almost totally involved with our own family concerns. A turning point in our prayer life came one Saturday morning in late October, 1972.

A truck pulled into our driveway. A man and woman who had been attending the church Carl pastored in addition to his teaching duties, came to the door and introduced themselves as Andrew and Darlys Himanga. Shyly they asked if they could talk with me. I invited them inside. After several false starts, it came out that they wanted to adopt a small child.

A load of ready-mixed cement had just been delivered, and Carl was pouring it in the basement, so he could not stop to join us. Andrew went downstairs to talk with Carl as he worked while Darlys sat down with me and told her story. The Himangas owned a large grain farm near Frederick, South Dakota, homesteaded by their Finnish ancestors. They wanted children desperately, but clinical tests indicated they would not have any of their own. This hurt because there would be no one to leave their property to when they were gone. Since both were approaching 40, they could find no adoption agency which would take their application. Darlys so yearned for children that she occasionally "borrowed" her sister's to pour out the love bottled up inside her.

I felt led to tell Darlys about my ruptured appendix and how resulting gangrene had so damaged my internal organs that doctors said I could not conceive and that if I did there would be a deformed child. Then I called April in and showed her my miracle child, born six years after this experience. April then went back outside to play in her tire-seat swing under the cyprus tree.

I took Darlys' hand. "Do you believe in miracles?"

She did not answer.

"I do not know of any baby available for adoption," I continued. "But I do know the power of prayer in Jesus' name. He can create a baby in your own womb."

When tears glistened in her soft brown eyes, I took both of her hands in mine and boldly prayed, "Heavenly Father, I ask You in faith to give Darlys and Andrew a child of their own. You made it possible for Sarah to bear a child for Abraham when no one believed it could happen. Please do the same for Darlys. I ask this in the name of Jesus, Your Son, Amen."

In the days that followed, Carl and I prayed for the Himangas. We put their request on a three-by-five card. I did not see Daryls again until Christmas time, two months later. I was playing the organ postlude at the close of a church service on Sunday morning. Almost everyone had left the church when I saw Darlys come toward the organ where I was talking with several friends. Shyly she put a white envelope on the music rack and left. It was addressed to me, but I waited until I got home to open it up. It was a Christmas card with a picture of the Madonna and Child on the front in pale blue. Inside was this note:

Dear Betty,

I have good news for you. I missed my period again this month. My stomach is a little upset; that must be a sign. This is the best Christmas gift I could receive. I feel God has blessed me with a child. Praise the Lord. I am glad we didn't have to adopt.

Love in Christ
Darlys Himanga

I seldom cry, but I did then. In my hand was confirmation that God was answering my prayers, using Carl and me as a team to believe together for the miraculous and the impossible.

The following August I found a tiny miniature envelope in my mailbox. Inside was a pink birth announcement with handwritten comments:

My name is Bertha Helen Himanga
I arrived July 31, 1973 ! ! ! ! ! ! ! ! ! (Figure it out)
Weighing 6 lbs and 8¾ oz.
My parents: Mr. & Mrs. Andrew Himanga
My length   19 inches
My chest   13 inches
My head   13 inches

I counted back. Darlys had conceived just a few days after her visit with us. For the past four years, we have kept in touch. Two weeks ago, I received their latest family portrait. They have three beautiful children born in four years. Inside was a note. "Please quit praying for me. Tell God not to overdo it!"

My prayer for the Himangas was not just an important milestone in their lives but in mine as well. I had been too self-centered in my prayers. God was directing me to the needs of others. I sensed too that the more concern I had for others, the quicker and more conclusive would be His answers to my troubles. My prayer life began to settle down along the following guidelines:

1. *Pray early and often.* When I first awaken in the morning, I talk to God before I even talk to my husband. The last thing I do before falling asleep, after kissing my husband good-night, is pray silently. I call it the "Oreo Cookie Concept." I start the day with prayer, end it with prayer, and the Lord fills the in-between with His joy, His love and His guidance.

2. *Prayer concentration.* Usually I close my eyes so as not to be distracted by things around me. I often kneel. For me, "kneeling is humility in form." I picture God through Christ. Once I saw a college professor writing out a grocery list while the minister was praying. That's sacreligious, I thought. Instantly, I felt a finger pointing at me. *Why were your eyes wandering?* How many times had I started to pray and then let my mind wander on such matters as: *Did I take any meat out of the freezer to thaw for dinner? Did I raise the flag*

on the mailbox when I put the letter in? Did I send the blue skirt to the cleaners? What rudeness! Did I expect God to keep His attention holding on me while I dabbled in trivia?

3. *Forgive someone.* Jesus told us our prayers won't be answered if we have "aught against any."

I forgave a businessman for shorting me $9,000 when my husband died.

I forgave the doctor who made the wrong diagnosis which resulted in my appendix rupturing. When I had a "glimpse of eternity" during the resulting hospital experience, followed by a complete healing, I was too glad to be alive to bring suit against him.

4. *Expect.* I pray with expectancy. In the process I'm discovering that prayer is not conquering God's reluctance but laying hold of His willingness. He loves; He wants me to be fulfilled. He isn't going to give everything I ask, but that doesn't mean I should ever stop asking and expecting.

The beginning of anxiety in me starts the decline of my faith. When my faith sags, it is almost impossible for me to pray with expectancy. Then I seek God alone, ask His forgiveness for my doubts, admit my helplessness without Him and then my cup begins to fill with the water of faith.

Sometimes in the expecting, we get so close to our need we cannot really believe. My friend, Lois Mitchell, and I were both in this condition several years ago. My need then was a husband. After six years I had given up. Her need was the healing of her husband, Bernard, who had a serious heart condition. For months he could not work or even climb stairs. We were so close to our situations we decided to trade prayers with "real expectancy" for each other.

And so each day I got on my knees with the focus on Bernard. I saw the love of Jesus surrounding him. I pictured Christ's healing hand placed gently on Bernard's heart. Then I visualized the heart muscle and tissue being revitalized, the red blood pumping more freely throughout his body. I saw all the parts of his body receiving this life-giving blood just as parched summer foliage drinks up a soaking rain.

As I forgot my own desires in my concern for Bernard, and as Lois pursued the same course for me, a spiritual law was at work. *Give, and it shall be given unto you; good measure, pressed down, shaken together, and running over* . . . (Luke 6:38).

Weeks and months passed. Bernard began improving, Lois reported. I met and married Carl Malz. Then several months ago Lois wrote that an amazing report had just come from the doctor. Bernie had passed his stress test and there was "no defect whatever in heart or arteries and no more medication was necessary!"

5. *Be willing to wait.* I often try to hurry God. It never works. His timing is always best for us. Yet I never seem to learn. A gas station attendant recently gave me a good lesson in patience. I had roared up to the pump on my way to the airport. "Fill it up. And hurry!" I shouted. He looked at me calmly and said, "Lady, there's no speed set on this pump. Just relax and turn off your motor. When it's full, the pump will shut off, and I will remove the nozzle. You can't leave until I put the cap back on your tank anyway."

I see now that the bumpy start in our marriage was good for Carl and me. When neither of us could get the other straightened out to our liking, we turned helplessly to God. Our extremity was His opportunity. When we began praying together, answers started coming. Carl's note to me on our fourth wedding anniversary brought tears to my eyes.

Dear Eve,

Yesterday Paul Davidson (a fellow teacher) said to me, "Betty is someone special to you isn't she? A light comes into your eyes every time you mention her name!" "Yes, she is," I replied. "There's only one like her in the whole world."

Honey, on this our fourth anniversary I feel "We've Only Just Begun!" I heard this song on the radio early this A.M. Like the people of Israel who existed as a nation for years, but who with the passover, were told, "This shall be unto you the beginning." I love you very much!

Adam

For some time I sat in a chair with gratitude in my heart holding Carl's note. In the world's eyes we were incompatible. But God's word to us was to ignore the world's opinion and keep our eyes on Him. I prayed we could continue to do this.

4

PRAYER FOR
WISDOM AND GUIDANCE

WE HAD A DECISION to make. Carl had just finished his four-year teaching contract at Trinity College and had received an invitation to come to Pasadena, Texas (just outside of Houston) and be considered as pastor for a wonderful group of people in a lovely church. We asked God to help us make the decision to go to Texas or stay at Trinity for another four years. I was torn. Brenda and Connie had both found their life's mates there in North Dakota, were happily married now and within easy visiting range. I did not want to leave "Whispering Pines," our old Spanish house on 38 acres with a pond and 300 pine trees.

The idea of living in a parsonage and being the wife of a pastor did not appeal to me. As a child I had lived in manses and watched my mother scrimp and save and sacrifice as a pastor's wife should and often must. I detested the on-stage, good-example, "goldfish bowl" existence. The fact that Carl was an ordained minister and a returned missionary was, I admit, one of the reasons I resisted marrying him. He allayed my fears when he told me he was no longer a preacher but a writer and teacher. Now it looked like I was being led into something I dreaded.

On the other side, my father and three brothers lived in Texas. If Carl accepted the pastorate, I would have a chance to see them more often.

Yet when we flew to Texas to be interviewed and look the situation over, my inner desire was overwhelmingly to stay where we were. The first night in Pasadena did nothing to change this. The area was dotted with refineries. Gulf, Texaco, Shell and Phillips Petroleum were all located there. The night sky looked like hundreds of Christmas trees lit up from the burning fumes.

"What is that smell?" I asked the man who was showing us around.

"What you smell, Honey, is money! Oil refinery fumes. It's hard on the eyes and lungs but easy on the pocketbook."

A look at the parsonage was only slightly reassuring. It was a pleasant, eight-room brick house. Yet 32 feet from the master bedroom was a busy road on which motorcycles roared by every night.

By now I knew I wasn't to trust my feelings as Carl and I prayed about this decision early each morning. We sought God's help, using as a basis the passage in James 1:5, "If any of you lack wisdom, let him ask of God, that giveth to all men liberally, and upbraideth not [doesn't make fun of]; and it shall be given him."

Before church the next morning the committee chairman asked me if there was anything I would want done to the parsonage. I could not believe the words I was hearing from my own lips, "We have prayed for God's guidance concerning this move. If the church votes to call my husband as pastor after having 39 other applicants, the parsonage will suit me fine."

My husband's sermon was titled, "Elijah, the ravens will feed thee there." He explained to the congregation that God had told Elijah to go to the brook and make camp. Elijah could go anywhere else that he wanted to, but God had commanded the ravens to deliver what Elijah needed *there*—at that campsite. As children of God we must find out where our "there" is, and then God will send provision for us "there," too. Woe is me if I am not "there" where I am supposed to be. Woe is me if I go "there" and the move is not under God's direction. Then Carl concluded, "If this position is God's will for you and for us, we will have an unmistakable confirmation of this."

The members of the church voted unanimously that Carl become their shepherd. I felt all my objections dissolve in the quiet conviction that here in Pasadena, Texas, was our "there."

The decision was right in every way. During our three years in Pasadena, God blessed us by providing many lasting friendships among our people who were generous with salary, gifts and many kindnesses. On our first Sunday we had 51 in attendance; within months, there was an average of 300 to 400 attending. The location gave me a good setting for the writing of a book, for speaking and television appearances and for unprecedented opportunities to serve the Lord. Yet, if I had listened to my personal desires, I would have insisted Carl not accept this call. Thank God I listened to Him, not my feelings.

The experience of our call to Pasadena taught me to seek God's guidance in every possible situation. Once during a question-and-answer period following my speech to a group of college students at Moorhead State, a young man in a dark field jacket stepped forward and accosted me. "I don't believe that story about your death and return to life."

He was so hostile I breathed a quick prayer for help. Then I answered that my story wasn't unusual, that several accounts like mine appeared in the Bible, such as Lazarus and Dorcas, not to mention the resurrection of Jesus Christ.

"I don't believe in God, and the Bible is fiction," he retorted.

"If you don't believe in God, then of course you can't believe my story."

He looked at me intently. "Show me God. Introduce me to Him, let me shake hands with Him, and I'll believe in your God."

I prayed quietly. *Lord, if You don't give me an answer for this young man, I will remain silent rather than to give the wrong answer.*

"If you will wait until after the questions," I replied, "I will talk to you personally. Perhaps I can do something to help you."

He was sharp and quick, "If you really want to *help* me, see if you have two aspirins in your purse. I have a helluva headache."

The kids roared with laughter. The answer came from outside myself. "I don't believe you have a headache. I've never seen one. If you will introduce me to your headache and let me shake hands with it, I will believe you have one and buy you a whole box of aspirin."

The meeting broke up then in a good spirit, but the young man did not remain for a personal talk. As I left the auditorium I marveled at how the Holy Spirit handled this difficult confrontation through me—and by using humor.

One day I was in the Atlanta airport about to board my plane when I heard a woman call, "Betty, wait, just one minute!" Turning around I saw an attractive young woman, well dressed, but grossly overweight, hurry up to where I waited. "I've just read your book," she said. "In it you state that nothing is impossible with God. Do you have a suggestion to help me with my weight control? I've tried diets, pills, a psychiatrist and a hypnotist. They didn't help. What should I do now?"

Lord, what should I answer.

It came. "Try the Bible: Psalm 141, verse three: 'Set a watch O Lord, before my mouth, keep the door of my lips.' Write this verse down and read it every time you're tempted to snack or ask for a second helping," I told her.

As I found my seat on the plane, I was amazed at my answer. It was the same verse I had used years before to keep from lashing out at my mother-in-law when she criticized me. Yet it was just as appropriate for an over-eater. God's word is sharper than a two-edged sword, cutting in two directions.

Months later, I received a letter from this woman, written

to my publisher and then forwarded to my home. She had placed the verse from Psalms on the refrigerator door. It had served as a sentry posted at the door of her mouth, guarding her appetite, warding off temptation to over-indulge. She had lost 46 pounds and kept it off to the pleasure and amazement of her husband and family.

I am not suggesting through these experiences that prayers for God's guidance take the place of any program of basic education. Only that we supplement what we learn with the knowledge He can give us. There is a scripture (John 14:26) which states that "the Holy Spirit will bring all things to our remembrance," that when we need to provide someone with a word of knowledge, He will give us the answer and speak through us, teaching us what we should say.

My father coached me as a child, "Betty, learn all you can and do *your* best. Then pray and He will give you *His* best which will make up the difference."

While traveling to a prayer conference in Brockville, Ontario, I looked through some prepared notes I had made of things I wanted to say. Somehow they seemed inadequate. I prayed, "Lord, I don't want these to be just random thoughts; help me to offer prescriptions that will heal personal problems that come up at this conference."

That night in my motel room, in a kneeling position, my Bible open in front of me, I searched for one definite scripture and found it: Isaiah 57: "Peace for him that is far off (Canada is far off from Texas) and I will hear and heal him." "Peace after prayer" became my topic.

When I sat down at the speaker's table I noticed the decorating theme was a dove, the symbol of peace. How appropriate! Prayer had brought me guidance that was right on target.

In my talk I described how peaceful it is sitting alongside a calm river of water and quoted psalm after psalm. I then talked about the natural healing qualities of water and described my complexion problem at age 13. I had tried various remedies on my face with no results. I still had the pimples. When I visited a dermatologist, he said, "Drink six to eight full glasses of water each day."

It sounded too pat, too easy, but I did it. The water flushed the impurities from my system allowing my face to clear up.

The results of telling this one very simple illustration amazed me. A woman with a bladder infection that penicillin would not clear up, tried the water remedy. The infection was soon gone. Two people in the audience wrote to tell me that they had never been able to wear contact lenses. After drinking eight glasses of water per day, they had sufficient moisture in the eyes to wear contacts quite comfortably. A young woman with an embarrassingly dry vaginal tract, wrote to tell me that nothing had helped previously, but the water suggestion had given her complete and pleasant relief.

Mothers with as many as four teenage children have written that their young people have cleared up their complexion and skin problems as a result of drinking water. (It works about 85 percent of the time.) They can now eat chocolate as long as they keep up the water consumption. I am still getting mail from people with elimination problems who did not get enough help through laxatives but discovered that drinking water solved the difficulty.

If I had followed normal reasoning, I would have thought this water tip too small to mention to a large audience of people. The Holy Spirit is the perfect Prompter when you are about to speak to a group of people.

Several years ago I received three invitations to speak on the same day. One was from a Presbyterian Church which offered a generous honorarium; one was to speak to a businessmen's club, with a good honorarium which would be followed by an autograph party at a local bookstore; the third was for a fund-raising dinner in Los Angeles for Teen Challenge, the drug and alcoholic rehabilitation program for youth originated by David Wilkerson.

My natural inclination was to accept the invitation from the church. It was close to home. The other two involved long flights, and I avoid travel whenever I can.

I did what I am learning to do about every invitation: ask the Lord for His answer. Two days later I accepted the invitation from Teen Challenge of Los Angeles, then asked God to give me an outline and subject topic since He knew who would be attending. What came was the theme, "I had to die to learn how to live."

A young, 24-year-old woman came forward at the end, weeping with joy and excitement. "I had not planned to come here," she told me. "I have never gone to church. I have never read the Bible. I was pushing a grocery cart in the supermarket when a woman I did not know walked up to me and said she had bought a ticket to attend a luncheon where an author was to speak. Now she couldn't go. Would I go in her place? I would receive a very good meal and hear a speaker with a strange story. I don't know why I said yes, but I came."

At this point, she began laughing, crying and pumping my hand up and down saying, "No one told me that I would ever see Tommy again. I had no idea I would ever hold my baby boy again. I thought his little body would always be in the ground, and it was all over and ended forever."

When she quieted down, I learned the details. She and her husband were grieving over their only child, Tommy, a two-year-old who had died five months before. She admitted she had not been a good wife or housekeeper since. She had lost the desire to live, feeling that since his death she too wanted to die. She explained that at the point when I read in the Bible that in heaven "we would know as we are known," she had nearly jumped out of her seat.

How could she ever get to heaven? She was not religious. Then when everyone prayed together that Jesus would come into their hearts as Lord, she prayed for this as well. Suddenly she knew she would see and hold Tommy again. "I can't wait until my husband gets home from work today, and I can tell him what I've done—tell him that he too can see Tommy again. No one ever told us that Tommy would have a chance to live again. I feel as if I have just begun to live. I don't want to die now!"

Out of this same luncheon in Los Angeles, which the Lord clearly led me to accept, came one of the most supernatural answers to prayer in which I've ever been involved.

After the luncheon the last person to approach me was very secretive. "May I talk with you for just a few brief minutes—in private?" she asked.

The only place available was a small conference room into which several coat racks had been shoved, leaving space for only two chairs. She carefully closed the door and we sat down. "Call me Ruth, but please don't ask me my full name for my husband's sake," she began. "I'm trying to keep his awful secret."

She checked the door again and stood by the window, looking out. "My husband is a professor at a state college not far from here. He left me for another woman. My heart's breaking just like our broken home. I can't even cry any more."

She struggled for composure, then continued. "You said today, 'If you can trust, all things are possible.' Do you think prayer and trust would change not just a circumstance, but a mind . . . my husband's mind?"

"Yes, I do. The Bible tells how Jacob wrestled with an angel, and his nature was changed." Looking at Ruth, I found it hard to believe that a husband could desert her. She was poised, had a pleasant voice and an air of quiet elegance. The few silver grey strands that streaked her dark hair were actually highlighted by her silver earrings and neck chain which perfectly matched her dark plum, suede dress.

"For several months now, my husband has been living in an apartment with his young secretary," she continued. "I have kept his secret, thinking that he would soon come to his senses and realize that this girl is the same age as our married daughter, that he would see how foolish this fling really was. I do not want his students to know. They would lose confidence in him."

She sat down in the chair, clasping her hands together. "One morning this past week I was sitting alone in our breakfast room drinking a cup of coffee, watching the birds having their breakfast on the bird feeder. Suddenly my husband drove into the driveway. I was so glad that I had brushed my hair and put on the breakfast coat that he had so much liked. It has lilacs printed on it. While he was getting out of the car, I poured him a cup of coffee and placed it on the table next to mine. I tried to be cheerful when I let him in the side door.

"He merely stepped inside, shook his head when I asked if he wanted a cup of coffee. He just stood there, rigidly, and said, 'I'm glad you are up and awake. I was on my way to the school for my first class, and decided to stop instead of calling you on the phone. Debi is not satisfied with our arrangement. She wants a husband and children. Please file for a divorce on the grounds of adultery. It will make it easier for everyone.' When he left, I was so discouraged and upset I wanted to die."

I took her hand and squeezed it. "I can't help you," I said, "but I know Who can. We are going to pray to Him right now."

She nodded. "I would like that."

"Heavenly Father, You are the Healer of bodies and the Restorer of broken relationships," I prayed. "Please repair this marriage, restore it and replace this woman's sadness with joy. Make a bridge of Ruth's broken dreams and form a rainbow of all her tears. Clear up the confusion in the mind of her husband. Touch his heart, lead him to repentance. We pray this for Debi, too, that she see that the way to a home with children is not through stealing another woman's husband. Cleanse this whole situation, Lord, in the Name of Jesus."

The date of this speech was December 9. Ten days later, on December 19, in Houston, Texas, near my home, I was speaking at the Holiday Inn to a Christian Women's Club luncheon. My subject was Christmas prayers. Toward the close I stated that for Christmas, God would restore broken hearts, broken homes, give us the desires of our hearts if we would ask Him in prayer. This would be His present to us. When things are right between us and others, we will have *His presence* to make Christmas more meaningful than *presents.*

Then I prayed, "Lord Jesus, we feel Your power beginning to answer our prayers right now. If there is anyone here who has never received You, who needs Your forgiveness, who yearns for the life eternal You promise, nudge them now, Lord. Touch their hearts. Move them to a decision."

I opened my eyes at that point to see a shapely young woman in a pink jersey dress walking out the door. Since people rarely leave when someone is praying, I remember thinking that she probably was ill.

After the prayer, people remained in their seats for a few other remarks and Christmas greeting suggestions. I saw the young woman return, place her head down on her arms for a few minutes, then sit up. I was convinced that she had taken sick.

As I was leaving the banquet hall, I stopped to talk to one of the waitresses when this young woman who had walked out during the prayer came up to me. She waited until she had my full attention, and suddenly threw her arms around my neck and began to weep uncontrollably. Then she apologized for getting the front of my dress wet with her tears. When we had found two chairs alone at the side, she told me her story.

"I am home for the Christmas holiday visiting my parents. I had not planned to come to this luncheon. When I saw your picture in the paper, I remembered your book in a bookstore window at the college where I work in California. On a strange impulse I decided to come and hear your talk. I thought you would talk about your book."

She found it hard to go on and I, with a sudden inner

knowing, put my arm around her. Then she continued. "When you said that God would restore broken homes if we asked in prayer, I couldn't sit there any longer. I went out to the lobby and called long distance to my boss in California. I've been working as a secretary to a college professor. We became very close, and he moved in with me, promising to marry me.

"I guess I was terribly selfish because I didn't think about his wife until I was convicted by what you said. Well, I told him I was resigning as his secretary. I told him to go home to his wife and beg her forgiveness, then to ask God to forgive him, because that was exactly what I was going to do. I am going to stay here in Houston with my parents and get myself straightened out. I feel clean inside now. Thank you for waking me up. Thank you for teaching me about prayer."

Four days later I received a letter.

Dear Betty,

God has answered prayer in a mysterious way since you were here. Debi phoned a few days ago and turned my husband down, just plain dropped him and quit her job. Last night my husband came home and we talked about it for the first time.

Before going to bed, we knelt together and prayed with our arms around each other. God forgave him there. I had forgiven him days ago.

In bed, lying on his arm, he caressed my face and told me, "I almost came back on December 9th. But after ruining Debi's reputation I didn't have the nerve to tell her I had changed my mind. I also was afraid that you would not have me back." I asked him what caused him to change his mind. "I can't explain it. It was like I had been arrested by an unseen policeman and told, 'Go home!'" he said.

You're right. Nothing is impossible with prayer.

Thankfully,
Ruth

5

PRAYER FOR SMALL NEEDS

Anything large enough for a *wish* to light upon,
is large enough to hang a *prayer* upon . . .
George Macdonald

FOR MANY YEARS I directed my prayers toward the large and important things out of necessity. I thought that God must have a good sense of humor to put up with all the trifling "piffleberries" people threw at Him to solve. "Don't bother God with small things," I used to advise my Christian friends.

Mom Perkins, my paternal grandmother, was the first to change my thinking. "Betty, you have not because you ask not," she would say when I complained about our constant indebtedness during my marriage to John. "I talk to God about everything. I live alone and have no one else to talk to. If I have a need, I ask Him. If I can't find something, I look up and say, 'Lord, now tell me—where did I put that?' "

"But God gave us intelligence to handle the small matters," I protested.

My grandmother would just shake her head. "We need Him for all things. Once I couldn't find my nutmeg to put in an apple pie. I asked the Lord to find it for me. In exactly six minutes Mrs. Green was at my door. She said, 'Mrs. Perkins, I borrowed this nutmeg weeks ago and forgot to return it. Why, just this minute I remembered to bring it back.' "

Her creed for living was centered in the words of this song:

> Oh what peace we often forfeit;
> Oh what needless pain we bear.
> All because we do not carry
> Everything to God in prayer.

One day, I suddenly looked up at the clock to find I had just 20 minutes before my hair appointment. I was glad that Palmetto Coiffure was only a few minutes from my house, but I had promised Carl that I would mix up his favorite fruit salad and leave it in the refrigerator to marinate. In that way, when we both came in for lunch, it would be ready. I could prepare it now and make my appointment—if I hurried.

The salad included some cantaloupe, white seedless grapes and fresh or canned peach slices. When I reached into the crisper of the refrigerator, I learned that what I thought was a peach was an apple. What an irritating discovery at this late minute. I already had the white grapes and the cantaloupe cubes in the bowl. Remembering Mom Perkins, I said impulsively, "Lord, this is frustrating, especially since I promised Carl. Please tell me what to do."

Then I rushed off for the beauty parlor. Pat Priddy shampooed, set and combed my hair. When I stopped at the desk to pay for my permanent, the owner, Elsie Swan, gave me my change and then reached into her desk and said, "You've been such a good 'patient' today, I have a surprise for you." She pulled out and handed to me the plumpest, juiciest peach I had ever seen. I was awed. The beauty shop would be the last place to look for an answer to prayer.

While cutting up the peach for Carl's salad, two scriptures came to my mind: "The Father knoweth what you have need of, even before you ask" (Matthew 6:8). And, "It shall come to pass, that before they call, I will answer; and while they are yet speaking, I will hear" (Isaiah 65:24). Or put another way: "Ye have not because ye ask not" (James 4:2).

Children have little trouble receiving answers to prayer and less hesitancy in asking. We were preparing to go on a family trip that would take one month. Meanwhile our mare was due to give birth while we would be gone. The whole family was concerned. What if the mare had trouble in delivery? There were 38 acres of pasture. She might give birth in a remote spot with no one to attend her. What would happen?

Then April began to fret. "We won't know when it comes, or see it, or pet it until it's a month old. I'm going to pray that it will come early before we leave."

I cautioned her, "Don't pray against nature. God is nature. That colt must not come 12 days early to satisfy your selfish desire."

April thought a moment and said, "I'll ask God that it come in a natural way before we leave."

Sure enough, the mare did give birth to a colt 12 days early; it was fully developed and larger than the last colt born on our farm. We all enjoyed it for two days before we had to leave. Never underestimate the power of a child's prayer!

To be sure, prayers for the inconsequential can get out of hand or become ridiculous. I had a woman say to me, "Betty, pray that God will fill my teeth so I won't have to go to the dentist."

"I can't," I replied. "Your dentist is a close friend of mine. He asked me to pray that God will prosper his business and send him new patients so that he may better provide for his three daughters who are approaching college age."

There's the story of an eccentric old man who rose to his feet during a church meeting and very slowly and deliberately turned to face the people to praise God—for the killing of a mouse! "God can do anything," he said. "I couldn't sleep because this mouse in the closet made so much noise. I prayed, and it stopped chewing for a while and then started again. I prayed again, 'God, kill that mouse, so I can sleep.' And He did it! The next morning that gray mouse lay there in the closet as dead and flat as a pancake." He sat down.

His spunky little wife immediately rose to her feet. "Why you ol' fool, that weren't God. I killed that mouse myself with the heel of your own boot." She sat down.

Her husband popped up quickly and retorted, "Folks, that goes to show you that if you pray, God can use just any old thing at hand to answer yer prayer."

In meeting our small physical needs, God often answers two prayers with one action. While living in North Dakota Carl and I had to watch every penny. We needed firewood which cost $7.50 for a very small load. We could not afford that. I prayed, "Lord, help me to locate some fireplace logs that we can afford. Maybe we could even cut them ourselves."

Two days later Carl and I were at home when there was a knock at the door. A muscular young man about 35 years old introduced himself as a tree surgeon and informed us that our row of trees along the driveway needed trimming. We invited him in and got his estimate. He looked only mildly disappointed when we told him that we could not afford this work.

"You're a reverend, aren't you?" he asked Carl, shifting his feet uncertainly.

"Yes, I'm a pastor and a teacher," Carl replied.

"My wife left me for someone else. I drink a lot to try to forget. I need help. Could you . . . maybe pray with me?"

Carl and I knelt beside him in front of our black leather couch which had become our prayer altar. He poured out his grief, asked God's forgiveness for his sins—especially the bitterness and hatred. When he started to leave, his face was joyous and peaceful.

He shook hands with us both. "My men will probably wonder where I am. They're trimming in the city park. I sure hate paying the dump 50 cents for every load I throw out there."

Puzzled, I grabbed his arm. "The wood you cut is taken to the dump?"

"That's right. Do you need any firewood?"

In the next two days, he brought 26 truck loads of wood into our barn lot. Then he cut the branches into firewood and stacked it into piles that soon became mountainous. I looked to God and said, "Thank you for an overwhelming abundance."

Then came another small need: a desk of my own. Although a writer and columnist for some years, I had never owned my own desk. I had used my father's at home and my husband's since marriage.

There was one in the Montgomery Ward catalogue I particularly liked. I prayed, "Lord, help me earn the money in some way."

I submitted several free-lance articles to magazines, but they were rejected. Then I received an invitation to speak at a women's club. My faith mounted. This would be the source of supply for the desk payment. There were 320 women present, the meeting was successful, but my honorarium was only $9.16 over my car and travel expenses. What a disappointment!

When an invitation came shortly thereafter to speak at another church, I refused, saying I didn't want to be away from my family. Then I thought it over. I had to admit I was still annoyed at the low honorarium I received at the women's club. *Am I doing this for money or to help people?* After praying about it, I called the church back and accepted their invitation.

Several people came forward at the close of the service to accept Jesus as personal Savior. My joy was full. Forget money—this was pay enough. As I was leaving, the minister handed me an envelope. "Here is the love offering we took up in the collection plates," he said.

The following morning I got out the Montgomery Ward catalog. Then I poured the offering out on the bed and began counting. I could not believe my eyes. The total collection was 13 cents more than the payment needed for the desk. Wasn't that strange? No. The extra 13 cents was for the stamp to mail the payment in to Montgomery Ward office.

The Bible says, "My God shall supply all your *needs*, according to His riches in glory, by Christ Jesus our Lord." He had supplied the desk. That was a need: but was he concerned about wants? I believe so.

I was passing through Herberger's Department Store when the fragrance of Germain Monteil's Royal Secret wafted past my nose. It had been four years since I could afford any of these products. I started to leave the store, then returned and bought Royal Secret hand lotion and cologne for a total of $15.

Guilt struck as I was leaving the store. I didn't need these items. God promises to supply our needs, not wants. Fifteen dollars was a lot when we needed so many other things. Then another passage came to mind. "Delight thyself also in the Lord, and he will give thee the desires of thine heart" (Psalm 37:4). Now I was confused. "What is right, Lord? I want only to do that which is pleasing to You."

The answer came when I arrived home. My neighbor met me when I got out of the car and handed me a white envelope. "An elderly lady brought this to your door. When she found out you were gone she asked me to get it to you."

Thanking my friend, I opened the envelope and found a note. "This is for you personally, Betty. Do not spend it on groceries and essentials." Inside were a 10 and a five dollar bill.

On another occasion I was very homesick to see my daughter, Brenda, who was living with her husband in Columbia, Missouri. It had been more than a year since we had been together. But Brenda and her husband couldn't afford to visit us—nor we them.

I knelt and talked to the Lord, "You know how much I want to see my daughter. It is good and right for parents and their grown children to see each other at least once a year. Please help us find a way." The following evening a pastor by the name of Lon Calloway called and invited me to speak to his congregation, offering to pay expenses. I was not very enthusiastic until he told me the location of his church—Columbia, Missouri.

The visit with Brenda and Bud was all too short. I spoke in Mr. Calloway's church on Sunday morning, then returned with Brenda and Bud after the service to the motel to check out and head for the airport. As I did, the desk clerk handed me a white envelope. I opened it and read as follows:

Dear Betty:

We have just learned that your daughter lives here in Columbia. It would be a shame to leave after such a short visit. Please stay over another day at our expense in the motel; charge your meals and have a good visit. Please don't refuse us the privilege of doing this for you and for her. Consider it a cup of cold water in His name.

> Lovingly,
> Lon and Stella Calloway

Little touches and blessings are so deeply satisfying when they happen through Him. Sister Kathleen, director of St. Joseph Hospital in Mount Clemens, Michigan, asked me to speak at their annual prayer breakfast on a Monday morning. I was to give a talk at the Village United Presbyterian Church the Sunday night before. I packed a pink, rosebud-print dress, and took along a soft, rust-colored, two-piece jersey dress with gold accessories.

Before the Sunday evening service I had put on the rust outfit, but it felt wrong. "Lord," I prayed, "forgive me for thinking about little things when the people and what I will say are more important, but give me guidance in this little matter of what I am to wear." I changed quickly into the pink, rosebud dress. When we arrived at the church sanctuary, I sat on the front pew, in full view of the pulpit area before I was introduced, looking at the spot where I would be standing in a few minutes. At each side of the altar were candles and an urn containing tiny pink roses, just buds, in the center of fern arrangements: live flowers exactly matching those in my dress. When I had selected my clothes in Texas for the trip, I knew none of this, but as the scripture says, "He knoweth all things."

The following morning I wore the rust-colored dress as I stood at the end of the speaker's table meeting the resident doctors, nurses and hospital officers. Directly behind me was a 24-foot wall mural—an autumn forest scene of rust and gold leaves.

My husband's secretary received word that her father living in Panama City, Florida, was dying. Carl put her on the plane for Florida. After returning from the airport, he moaned, "What am I going to do? I need a typist immediately to meet a manuscript deadline." Together we prayed a simple prayer: "Oh God, you know where there is a fast, efficient typist. Help us find her." He left the house and I started my housework.

Twenty minutes later, I went outside to give water to our collie dogs. Missy was missing. I took the car and began scouting the neighborhood without results. Then it came to me that I should go home and wait for someone to phone me that Missy had been found. That didn't make too much sense because Missy did not have on a collar; hence no name tag, identification or number.

About two hours later, the phone rang. A new woman in our neighborhood who knew we had collies had found Missy. When I arrived at her house, I found her a charming, pleasant woman. She was also—a secretary! This woman not only was answer to two prayer requests but turned out to be the finest part-time help Carl has ever had.

Call it coincidence if you want, but there are four million people in the Pasadena-Houston area and freeways layered six levels deep. Missy could have been killed in the traffic or gone to any number of millions of other houses. There is nothing too big or small for God.

On another occasion, what started out as a prayer for a

small need set off a chain reaction of events which supernaturally affected the lives of many people, making this scripture live for us: "He is able to do above all that we ask or think" (Ephesians 4:20).

It began when I was invited to appear on the television show, "To Tell the Truth." One of the producers had read the article about me in Guideposts magazine and thought that my appearing as the woman who had been dead for 28 minutes would make an interesting show. The photograph of April Dawn with me in the magazine gave the producer an idea. At the close they would have April come out before the three women claiming to be Betty Malz and kiss the real one. I agreed to do it.

While preparing to leave for New York I realized my two pieces of unmatched luggage were falling apart. During my last trip, I had bound the blue one together with several layers of masking tape, praying that it would not fall open. Now I asked, "Lord, I do not have the money to buy new luggage. Please help with this, somehow."

At the Houston Intercontinental Airport, as we watched our patched-up luggage go off on the conveyor belt, April spoke up, "Why don't you pray for new luggage, Mother? You pray about everything else."

When I explained that I already had, she replied, "Well, I think we're going to get the answers to our prayers on that television program."

The TV show went smoothly. I appeared so ruddy with my Texas tan that I did stump the panel members. They thought I looked too healthy to have ever been near death and voted for one of the other two women. My prize—you guessed it—a set of gold American Tourister luggage.

Small miracle, yes, but the more deeply satisfying result of our appearance on this show came later. One of the men we met on the television set used my story as a prayer guide for a woman friend who had been seriously injured in an automobile accident and had stayed in a coma for weeks, much as I had done. He and his pastor prayed before this unconscious woman just as if she were conscious, believing that their words of comfort, hope and assurance would penetrate in a deeply healing way. Hours after this prayer, the woman came out of the coma and recovery began from that point. "The power of the Holy Spirit in a situation like this amazes me," he wrote me, telling of the recovery.

I'm discovering each day that God is in the small things of life as well as the large. He is teaching me simplicity and flexibility. There was the time I had dinner with old family friends, the Nagy family, in Clinton, Indiana. There were 11 of them: I made 12. We sat down and I expected someone to say a blessing. No one did. They ate, so I ate.

After everyone had finished, they all joined hands around the table, closed their eyes, and Mr. Gabor Nagy prayed, "Lord, we thank you for the tasty food we have just eaten and enjoyed. Thanks for providing it. Bless my good wife, Elsie, for fixing it. Bless my sons for helping to grow it. Now bless my girls as they do the dishes."

It was simple, it was different, it was beautiful.

6

THE ONE-WORD PRAYER

> Few delights can equal the mere presence of ONE whom
> we trust utterly.
>
> George Macdonald

MY MOTHER USED to play a game with us children when we
would ask her for something. She would answer, "What's
the magic word?"

"Please," came our reply.

"What's the password?" she continued.

"Pretty please, with sugar on it!"

Mother would grin and hand us what we had asked for.
As my knowledge of prayer has grown I've discovered that
there's an even more powerful word than "please."

I first learned it at the most critical stage of my life when
I was on the threshold of passing through the thin curtain
between this life and the next. At that point my father prayed
the shortest and most powerful prayer there is. He was at
my bedside in the hospital. A nurse had drawn a sheet over
my lifeless body. My father breathed one word with all the
passion and emotion he possessed.

"Jesus!"

I heard it, though I was far away. The prayer asked for
nothing. Yet it had supreme authority. I remember wanting
to stay in that lovely heavenly place, but the power in the

name of Jesus drew me back to the hospital bed. Seconds later my hand pushed the sheet off my head and the life processes began functioning again in my body.

Why is this one word prayer so powerful?

I don't understand very much about spiritual warfare, the battle for our souls waged between God's angels and the forces of Satan; but I do know that our best weapon is identified in the Bible: When with His disciples, Jesus prayed "Holy Father, protect them by the *power* of Your name—the name You gave me—so that they may be one as we are one" (John 17:11). Jesus also promised: "You may ask anything in My *name*, and, I will do it" (John 14:14).

An elderly lady we all lovingly called Grandma Rice discovered this power some years ago in Vincennes, Indiana. As she tells it, "The prayinest prayer I ever did pray was standing on my head in a well. I was cutting across a field to pick wild blackberries to make jelly. I stepped on the rotten wooden cover of an old open well. The boards snapped, and I pitched headlong into the dark water below. As I struck the water I remember feeling total panic. I couldn't swim or tread water. I prayed just one word: 'Jesus.'"

In the next field was a man plowing a cornfield. Here's the story he told: "I had been plowing for a half hour or so when I heard the words, 'Turn off the motor.'

"There was no one around and I was sure my mind was playing tricks on me. Then it came again—an insistent inner voice: 'Turn off the motor now.'

"I did so and heard a splash and a muffled cry. I ran toward the sound, saw the well and grabbed an old rope lying by the broken well curb. It had probably been used years ago to draw buckets of water. I lowered it into the well. The girl who had fallen into the water was choking and coughing, but she grabbed the rope and I was able to pull her up."

Once again the power in the one-word prayer, "Jesus," summoned heavenly aid. Supernatural forces seem to spring into action when the Name of the "most beloved Son" is called.

Geronimo, a large, gentle, white gelding horse, belonged to Brenda when we were living in Florida. Brenda could do anything to him or with him: braid his tail, hold onto it while he pulled her around the pasture (which I don't recommend). Brenda would lie across his back and play dead and he would bring her carefully home from a little friend's house down the road. More than once when April was just learning to walk, she would make a break when we were holding her hand and walk under Geronimo. The gentle horse would hold quite still, never moving until we pulled April away. One day I looked up and a neighbor's child was sitting under Geronimo to get out of the hot sun. He was a very gentle horse indeed with children.

Then something happened to Geronimo. He started chewing the top rail off the fence. We had to replace it twice. He ate clothing from off the clothes line, especially diapers.

One day, I took April's hand and she toddled alongside me to say hello to old Geronimo. He stretched his neck, reached down with his teeth, picked April up by her little yellow checked dress, and ran off like he was crazy, running in circles, wagging her from side to side between hundreds of skinny pine trees in the pasture. He was eating her little dress, right down to the collar band around her tiny neck, as he ran. I screamed at him, I yelled at the neighbors for help, then jumped the fence to go after the demented horse. Just as I reached him I moaned softly, "Jesus."

Geronimo stopped dead still at this command, let April down slowly, and stood there quietly.

I picked up April, wondering if her skull could have been crushed against one of the trees. All I found on her was green grass stain mixed with saliva. Sadly I called the vet to come and dispose of poor old Geronimo. After a thorough check-up the vet gave us his report: the old horse had a mineral deficiency in his system and was supplementing his diet with the dyes from the strange things he was eating. He needed red mineral salt. Geronimo was his old gentle self after the diet deficiency was handled; we kept him for years.

Since that experience, the dynamic single-word prayer has been the cornerstone of this mother's prayer life. And not without some opposition. There are those to whom the word "Jesus" is offensive. "Why not call out to God?" they ask. "After all God is the Supreme Being."

I tell such people that of course prayers to God are effective and answered, that if they feel more comfortable praying to God alone, that's fine. But they should carefully examine themselves for the reasons they resist Jesus, or resist using His name. God Himself is the One who placed the mantle of authority on His Son, granting to Him all power through the heavenly forces at His command. It's as if the very mention of the name alerts these forces much as a bugle call has stirred soldiers to heights of strength and courage on the battlefield.

The one-word prayer is more than a crisis prayer. My neighbor once experienced cleansing through it. Jay and his wife, Helen, were a lovable couple—separately, that is. You could have a great time with either one of them apart from the other, but when together, they became quarrelsome and unpleasant. Jay was the owner of his own rig and tractor and hauled for TransAmerican Van Lines. He made good money and enjoyed being on the road away from Helen. She was extremely jealous of him.

When they moved next to us I prayed, "Lord, help me to help them." I soon discovered that Jay had a tender heart but could hardly talk without using four-letter profanities. Soon I was keeping my daughters away from him.

One day when my mother was visiting he came into our yard. In his conversation out spilled a four-letter word. Mother, in her quiet way said, "Jay, I wouldn't have in my hand what you just had in your mouth!"

Jay was angered at first, then crestfallen under the gentle reproof from my mother.

"What can I do, Mrs. Perkins? It slips out before I know it," he finally admitted.

"I've two suggestions, Jay. First, start going to church with us, and you'll pick up a different set of words. Second, each time you start to say that word, pause first and whisper the name, 'Jesus,' to yourself. Then if your word has to come out, let it."

"I'll try both," he promised.

Jay and Helen did start coming to church. One Sunday Jay knelt at the altar and surrendered his life to the Lord. He told mother afterwards, "It works. Jesus now guards my tongue. He is also the center of my life. If only Helen would join me." But his wife was not interested in making such a commitment, she told him.

On one of his trips, Jay brought me a 10-pound bag of soft, papershell pecans from Georgia. I made a pecan pie and invited them to come over for dinner one summer evening. Later Helen and I saddled up the horses and went for a ride. At the back pasture we stopped in the soft twilight to let them graze, dropping the reins while we talked.

Helen had a short fuse, was quick to anger, and her husband instinctively answered her in kind. A few weeks before, during a quarrel, she picked up a hurricane lamp and broke it over his right knee. He almost bled to death before he got to the emergency room of the hospital.

Sitting there in the saddle, Helen let the whole story unwind. Jay had married her because she was expecting his child, and she had always felt that he did not love her enough to have married her otherwise. Temper flares, criticism and resentments had built up a wall of hostility between them. Helen had once left her hair in pink foam curlers for four days without taking them out. She admitted she had lost interest in herself, Jay and their small child. Now the tough exterior collapsed, and she began to cry.

"I confessed my sins to our pastor years ago, but he didn't do anything about it," she sobbed. "I just feel dirty about the whole thing."

I suggested that she could pray to God for herself right there on horseback.

"But, Betty, I don't know how to pray," she said sadly.

"Then let me pray for you," I said. "If I say something you don't agree with, stop me."

She looked relieved and told me to go ahead.

"Jesus, there is power in Your name to heal Jay and Helen's home life," I prayed. "Forgive Helen for the sin of fornication before her marriage to Jay. Help her to forgive herself. Move into her heart, Lord, so that she will know how much You love her."

When Helen thanked me for the prayer, I took another step and asked her to repeat after me a verse of scripture, "Let the words of my mouth, and the meditation of my heart, be acceptable in Thy sight, O Lord, my strength, and my Redeemer" (Psalms 19:14).

When we returned to the house, I showed it to her in a Bible which I gave to her to take home and keep. She started going to church with us, even when Jay was on the road. One Wednesday night during a testimony service, she stood to her feet, turned white with self-consciousness, but managed to stammer: "The word and name Jesus has been my editor for weeks now. I used to curse Jay and think up hurtful things to say to him. I started saying the name 'Jesus,' silently first before answering my husband. My speech has changed. Then I read in the Bible a friend gave me, 'Blessed are the peacemakers,' and I decided to be one. Jay and I don't quarrel now."

As Jay and Helen grew in their love for God, their daughter and each other, one song became their favorite which they requested the congregation to sing over and over. It was:

> My heart is stirred whene'er I think of Jesus
> O blessed name which sets the captive free
> The only name through which I find salvation
> No name on earth has meant so much to me.

The name of Jesus has been vilified, scorned and blasphemed for nearly 2,000 years. While He is a loving and patient Lord, I've discovered that there are times when He uses His power to openly rout the enemy. One such occasion took place in my father's church some years ago. The alcoholic father of a 17-year-old girl became annoyed with the church-going of his wife and daughter and boasted about town that he and his buddies might just kill the preacher and burn the church down. My brothers and I wondered why my dad was not afraid. When we pressed him, he said, "God can dispatch angels who are more than a match for any group of bullies."

I almost wished the bullies would attack so I could see a real tough angel in action. Instead the girl's father came alone to church one Sunday night near the close of the service. We heard the commotion at the back when the daughter and her mother were both kneeling at the altar in a rededication service at the close of my father's sermon.

Roaring drunk, the man burst through the door, shouting obscenities. When an usher moved toward him, the reeling man hurled him aside. Then, spotting his daughter and wife down front, he staggered toward them, waving his fist.

Sitting next to my mother in a pew on the fourth row, I was terrified as the enraged man brushed ushers and officials aside. Then I heard my mother breathe one word in strong confidence: "Jesus."

The drunk careened up the aisle and reached his cringing wife and daughter at the altar. As he leaned down and grabbed his daughter's wrists to jerk her up, we heard a scream. At first I thought it was the girl. Instead, it was her father. He slumped to the floor, moaning, staring at his *two badly burned hands*. Then completely sober, he slunk out of the church. I heard later it took weeks for the second degree burns on his hands to heal.

On the way home Daddy said he had seen the same thing happen once before. An enraged husband stormed into church intending to drag his wife out forcibly. When he grabbed his wife, the man's arms were badly burned all the way to his elbows.

The Holy Spirit can burn as well as heal.

In the summer of 1977, my husband, Carl, was invited
to return to Bangalore, India, for the Silver Anniversary Jubi-
lee of the Southern Asia Bible College, of which he had been
president. He was gone for one month, also visiting Egypt
and Russia.

Someone, knowing that he was away, began calling me
all hours of the night: sometimes once, but as many as four
times in one night. In a large city like Houston, such calls
are hard to trace.

One night I took the phone off the hook to get a full
night's sleep, then decided I shouldn't do that in case Carl
needed to get hold of me. Shortly after two in the morning,
the phone rang, arousing me from a sound sleep. I answered,
but there was no reply, just heavy breathing and sighing.
"Who is this?" I asked angrily.

Then a heavy, husky voice asked, "Can I come over? Is
your daughter home too?"

I started to hang up, then I remembered. Softly, but with
all the intensity I could muster, I said the one word: "Jesus."

Click. The receiver banged down. The man never called
back.

One night I was home alone at night awaiting my husband's
return from work. The children were in bed. I heard footsteps
outside and looked up thinking my husband was grinning
at me through the screen of the open bedroom window. Then
I froze. A strange man's face was staring back at me while
he pried at the frame around the screen.

Did I have time to call for help on the telephone? No.
He would be through the screen before I could dial the number. So I took a much better tack. I faced the intruder directly
and spoke aloud to him the full command. "In the name
of Jesus I rebuke you."

The intruder was startled and fell back into a pile of wood.
Then he got up and ran. I was awed. The man seemed to
have been jerked backwards by an invisible force. He fled
as if he had seen a ghost.

With chills running up my back I thanked Jesus for the

power in His name and for the help He provided through—what? An angel? It made sense somehow. The Bible promises this angelic help. Why do we doubt?

Would we not be overwhelmed if our spiritual eyes were opened and we could see how many times guardian angels are circling around us to keep us from harm—even when we don't even know we are in danger?

I did some research in the scriptures and came up with solid confirmation. God's word says that Jesus could have called thousands of angels to rescue Him from the cross if He had wanted to (Matthew 26:53).

How powerful and how strong is an angel? "The angel of the Lord went out and put to death a hundred and eighty-five thousand men in the Assyrian camp [in answer to Hezekiah's prayer]" (Isaiah 37:36, NIV).

In Psalm 103:20, David said God's angels "excel in strength."

In Psalm 34:7, we are told "The angel of the Lord encampeth around about them that fear Him, and delivereth them."

In I Chronicles, chapter 21, David lifted up his eyes and saw the angel of the Lord stand between heaven and earth having a drawn sword in his hand stretched out over Jerusalem. Judgment fell, and 70,000 of the enemy died.

In the book of Daniel, chapter six, verse 22: "My God hath sent His angel, and hath shut the lions' mouths . . ."

I love the comforting thought in Psalm 91, verse 11, "For He shall give His angels charge over thee, to keep thee in all thy ways."

One of the most remarkable stories of "invisible help" happened to Jack and Jenny Pate. Jack, a muscular trucker, and his dainty, southern-belle wife inherited an old house near Galveston, Texas, from Jenny's mother. They decided to take some time to fix it up before moving in.

One hot summer day Jack and Jenny arrived at the old house to do some wallpapering in an upstairs room. They brought their three-year-old daughter, Peggy, with them. The window was opened for ventilation. Peggy began playing among the wallpaper scraps, dropping little bits of paper from the upstairs window, watching as they were caught by the current of the breezes to flutter and swirl to the ground.

The sight so fascinated Peggy that she began to lean farther and farther over the sill.

Jack happened to look up at the very moment his little Peggy tumbled out the window.

"Oh, Jesus!" he moaned.

Beneath the window was a cement patio with three concrete steps having sharp protruding corners leading up to the door of the house. The thought of their daughter's body striking hard concrete from a second-story window paralyzed both Jack and Jenny with horror.

Then together they almost exploded down the stairs to reach the crumpled little body. Sobbing, they burst through the front door.

There sitting on one of the concrete steps, her little hands folded in her lap, was Peggy. Looking up she softly whispered, "Don't worry Daddy and Mommie, that big man caught me."

Dumbstruck they hugged their child, then with joy and relief Jack looked about to thank the man who had saved their daughter. It was an open country area, and he couldn't have gone far. But there was no one in sight!

Jenny hugged her daughter tearfully, then Jack picked Peggy up and carried her inside. Together they stripped off her clothing to examine her, laying her on the kitchen table. There was not even a pink spot on her little body where she could have landed or fallen.

The whole family talked of nothing else for some time, marveling, speculating. Nonbelievers were convinced that the "man" who caught Peggy had for some reason disappeared. The others believed the answer lay in Isaiah 63:9 ". . . the angel of His presence saved them, in his love and in his pity he redeemed them; and he bare them, and carried them. . ."

In all these experiences the one common denominator was the presence of Jesus. Today with the forces of evil running wild throughout the world, we need His power and His presence more than ever before.

Prayer in the name of Jesus is the "Royal Password" by which we turn the key that swings open the gates to the holiest of holies. This is where Jesus our intercessor sits at the right hand of God, making intercession for *us*. He provides the only visa or ticket to enter His court where decisions are made and miracles originate.

And as spiritual warfare builds to a climax, we are told in Paul's letter to the Philippians (2:9–11): "Therefore God exalted Him to the highest place and gave Him the name that is above every name, that at the name of Jesus every knee should bow, in heaven and on earth . . . and every tongue confess that Jesus Christ is Lord, to the glory of God the Father" (NIV).

7

DANGEROUS PRAYER

BE CAREFUL WHAT you pray for, you may receive it.

When I was 13 a distraught woman named Midge arrived at our house one evening just as Mother and I were leaving to walk to the post office. I heard her tearfully say something to my mother about a fight she had just had with her new husband. Seeing that my little brothers were listening with lively interest, Mother suggested Midge join us on our walk.

As we strolled along the sidewalk, the new bride exclaimed, "I think I'll just kill myself, then he'll miss me and find out he really loves me." Looking upward she dramatically cried, "Lord, I just want to die!"

Seconds later a car speeding around the corner, jumped the curb, struck a telephone pole, snapping it off at the ground. The pole fell only a few feet from us as we leaped aside to save our lives.

Midge screamed, "Oh God, I didn't mean it!"

At 13 this incident left one indelible truth on my young mind: Be careful what you ask of God.

When my father visited us recently, I was wrestling with the subject of dangerous prayer. "Daddy, you have followed the Lord closely and conscientiously for 48 years now. Have you ever asked, even nagged God for something and then have it turn out to be bad for you?"

My father chuckled. "We are told to ask, seek and knock.

But if we keep knocking and knocking on the wrong door long enough, the devil—not the Lord—may open it."

Then he told me that at one point in his career as a pastor he saw a lovely stone church in another community with matching Bedford stone parsonage. He looked at it with real desire. The congregation needed a pastor since theirs had recently resigned. It was located near a lake in a very prestigious area. He submitted his application and resume and prayed that God would let him be their pastor.

It wasn't that his own church was unsatisfactory. He had felt fulfilled where he was, his congregation was growing in maturity and numbers, and his family was contented. But the grass really did seem greener on the other side of the fence, about 85 miles to the north.

Dad was persistent in his prayers and contacts with the pulpit committee. He was finally called, and we made the move.

"Betty, it was the most miserable two years of my life," he said. "My desire had blinded my good judgment. I had not bothered to find out why the last minister had resigned. It was because the congregation was unresponsive and argumentative. Your mother became almost ill from the lack of love and warmth. Despite all my efforts, church attendance actually declined. The whole experience was frustrating."

The story of Heather Adams represents the most vivid example I know as to what can happen when we pray too hard and selfishly for something—or someone. Heather was so likeable that the whole community grieved when her husband, Jack, was killed in Vietnam, leaving her alone to rear a young son and daughter. We who loved her watched prayerfully while she struggled for a year to rise above grief, be a comforting mother to her children and get her personal affairs and life reoriented to widowhood.

Months later Heather met Ron and fell in love with him. On the surface they seemed to be a good match—both were such attractive people. Heather was vivacious, good-humored and courageous. Ron was suave, attentive to Heather's children and had faultless manners and dress.

Fear of a life of widowhood made Heather over-zealous for marriage and unwilling to hear the warning signals during the courtship. She told me later that Ron seemed more interested in her friendship than in physical contact. Once he admitted being hurt by a woman and had determined not to fall in love again. He doubted, he said, if he could ever again love any woman.

Heather took that as a challenge. "I determined that I had what it took to heal his broken heart," she told me. "I was claiming that verse, 'If you ask anything in my name, I will do it' " (John 14:14, RSV).

If I had known how intently Heather was applying that verse I would have warned her, but only later did she tell me the details. For weeks she read it very day. "I touched that verse, I rubbed it, and I quoted it aloud when no one was around. Then I prayed, 'Lord, I want Ron for my husband. He seems disinterested, but You can answer any prayer.' "

Ron began to call Heather regularly on the phone, then dined her. "I loved everything about him," she said. "Everything but his strange attitude of depression. I knew I could fix that, however. I would love him to a life of joy and laughter like Jack and I had known."

Heather said she fasted and prayed once for three days, begging and pleading with God, "Your word says it. Give me Ron for my very own." She did not ask God for His plan. "I merely zeroed in on that one verse like a bulldog; I sank my teeth into it. I dug my heels in and refused to give up. If God tried to speak to me, I didn't hear Him. My ears were deaf because my eyes told me that Ron was the one I desired and craved." Ron finally proposed.

Heather ignored every sign or check that came along. The day they were to go for blood tests, a sudden storm came up and the trip had to be postponed. The second time they nearly had a wreck on the way to the public health center. An elderly friend tried to tell Heather that Ron was too quiet and withdrawn, that she should wait until she knew him better.

All seemed to go well during the marriage ceremony. Heather looked radiant. Ron was his usual debonaire self. Then they went away on a honeymoon.

Weeks later I stopped in to see Heather. It surprised me somewhat to see that Ron seemed quite content to move into the home that Heather and Jack had shared for so many happy years until his death. Heather greeted me at the door warmly, but within minutes I knew something was wrong. Her eyes were dead, her shoulders drooped. She offered me a cup of coffee and we sat in her kitchen and talked.

In the middle of a sentence Heather stopped and stared at me with a sudden flush in her face. "Betty, I need to ask you something. What do you know about oral sex?"

I was startled. "Almost nothing," I said, trying to focus on a totally unexpected subject.

"Is it true that every couple does it?" she asked.

"Who told you that?"

"Well . . ." Heather hesitated, then just stared out the window.

Choosing my words carefully, I continued. "Heather, I've been married to two very virile men. Sex with them has been beautiful and completely satisfying without oral sex."

"The same with Jack and me," she said wistfully. Then abruptly she changed the subject.

When I shared the conversation that evening with Carl, he was thoughtful, even somber. "This generation has been getting a blast of propaganda about oral sex through x-rated films and the new sex magazines. But just because many people practice it, doesn't make it right. To me it's not normal; it's a kind of lust—lusting after the flesh."

"Would you be willing to say that to Ron?"

"I sure would if he would ask me for advice. I don't know that I can go to him and hit him cold on the subject."

"It's destroying their marriage. Heather looks just awful. All the life has gone out of her."

"I think there must be other problems too, Betty. She certainly has enough character to deal firmly with Ron on something like this."

Weeks went by before I saw Heather again. Then she called and asked to see me. Her voice was tense and low on the phone. When we met at a shopping mall, I listened as her woes poured out in a flood.

"Betty, I'm having such a difficult time with Ron. I've tried not to compare him with Jack, but Jack was comfortable and wholesome, and Ron is so unsatisfied and, well, odd." Heather looked at a display of women's shoes with unseeing eyes.

"Two weeks after the honeymoon," she continued, "I realized I had been like a little kid, racing down the stairs on Christmas morning, finding a large, beautifully wrapped package under the tree. But when I opened the package, it was empty." Tears filled her eyes. "Ron told me that he was unhappy because he was badly in debt and had kept it from me. I took a large amount of my government insurance from Jack's death policy, and he used it to pay off his debts. For two days he was like a set-free kid. Then came more depression. After a long talk, I learned that he had been married before. That was a blow, but I accepted his explanation that she was not a good wife.

"He got angry when I sent some valentines out to my parents and a few friends. He said I did it without his permission. One night he opened the Bible and read me the passage in Ephesians where it says that a woman must obey her husband in all things. He told me that he needed oral sex to be happy, that even if I felt it was wrong, he would face God for us both, but I was sinning because I would not obey him. He told me that all couples were doing it now and I was being a prude."

Heather turned and faced me. "That's why I asked you

the question, Betty. I just couldn't do it and told him so. But I wondered if I was too religious and not knowledgeable enough. So I told Ron I would pray about it. And I did; I told God that I loved Ron and that if he wouldn't change, then perhaps God should change me. I told God I would leave it up to Him.

"I began to study the Bible, Betty. Then weeks went by and Ron did not change. I took that same verse in my Bible, the one that was actually worn through the paper from my fingers rubbing it, and I read and reread it and prayed. I asked that since Ron hadn't changed his feelings about sex, was he right and I wrong?"

Heather faced me directly again. "I didn't get a yes or no from the Lord," she continued. "But I did get a sudden nostalgia for the warm, loving, very natural physical relationship Jack and I had experienced in our marriage. That was a good enough answer."

About 10 days later I had a telephone call from Heather. She was deeply upset. "Ron and I went to a psychiatrist," she began. "He told me I was a 'babe in the woods, an ostrich with my head in the sand.' He said we should do whatever brought us pleasure whether it was extramarital sex, premarital sex or homosexuality—as long as both parties consented. He then gave me a medical and psychiatric journal to study. It states that if two mature adults consent, they may indulge and exercise in physical sexual activity with another of the opposite sex or of the same sex."

This report shook me. I asked Heather for the name of the psychiatrist. Meanwhile, in answer to prayer, the Lord was bringing me in contact with other wives who were going through difficulties similar to Heather's.

One wife I counseled was despondent but couldn't seem to pinpoint the reason. For the first time in my life I asked the blunt question, "Do you practice oral sex?"

At first she flared, and I wondered if I had offended her. Then she sighed and slowly nodded her head. "I do, but I don't like it."

"Then why go on with it?"

"Because . . . well, Harry wants to."

"I'm discovering from wives like you that instead of bringing fulfillment, this kind of sex drains off joy and reduces vitality," I told her.

She agreed to talk it over with her husband. Within a week I had similar conversations with two other wives. Both had been swayed by arguments that it was modern, more erotic and more satisfying. Yet both admitted that it left them feeling dissatisfied.

One evening during casual conversation with one of our friends, a medical attorney, Carl learned that Heather's psychiatrist was a known, practicing homosexual. Carl said he feared that Ron was one too.

When I saw Heather again at her home there were deep shadows under her eyes. She confirmed Carl's and my suspicions. "Several days ago I became aware of the fact that Ron was lying to me about where he was spending one or two evenings a week. He was not playing tennis as he said, but going out with a young man who had been fired for homosexual behavior from a Christian college."

Tears began to trickle down her cheeks. "I confronted Ron and he admitted it, saying it was all my fault because I wouldn't do what he wanted me to do. When I told him I could no longer be his wife, he began pleading with me not to leave him. I agreed to stay only if he would get psychiatric help—but this time from a Christian psychiatrist."

Her shoulders began to shake and I held her hands in mine until she could continue.

"I asked Ron to kneel with me by the bed. And he did. I asked him to confess his sin and ask God for a cleansing. He couldn't do it. He only wept. He wanted sympathy but wasn't ready to change.

"The next morning Ron couldn't get out of bed to go to work. He was weak with fever. Our family doctor came at noon and gave him a shot. When I saw that the medication wasn't helping, I called a minister Ron knew and asked him to come and pray for Ron to be healed. Then I went into the bathroom, opened my Bible and read verses 14, 15 and 16 in the fifth chapter James."

I well knew the verses: "Is any sick among you? Let him call for the elders of the church; and let them pray over him, anointing him with oil in the name of the Lord: And the prayer of faith shall save the sick, and the Lord shall raise him up; and if he have committed sins, they shall be forgiven him. Confess your faults one to another, and pray one for another, that ye may be healed. The effectual fervent prayer of a righteous man availeth much."

"My heart leaped for joy at the words," Heather continued. "This was the miracle I could expect. This was God's grace and mercy making a way of escape, of rescue for Ron. This was why he became sick; it would be the door to the way out! For the first time in nearly a year I could see the light at the end of the tunnel. There would be no need for separation or for people to ever know about his past! I could hardly wait for this minister to arrive. I knew he was a Godly man who loved people."

Heather's voice broke, and it was several minutes before she could continue. "When the pastor came, Ron greeted him warmly. We talked generally for a while, then the pastor took a small bottle of olive oil from his pocket. He explained that he related this type of healing prayer to Jesus' suffering on the Mount of Olives where He spent the night in prayer, sweating great drops of blood. Before He went to the cross, Jesus was beaten on His back 39 times with a whip; we were to consider these 39 stripes as each representing 39 categories of major illnesses, each of which the power of Jesus can heal today."

She went on to tell how the pastor removed the lid from the bottle of oil, put a little on his forefinger and started to place it on Ron's forehead. Ron's face suddenly contorted. He knocked the bottle out of the pastor's hand, spilling it all over the bedspread. Then he took hold of the minister's wrist and said, "The same scripture that tells you to anoint with oil to heal the sick, also says to *call* for the elders. It won't work because I did not call you; Heather did."

The minister stepped back, bowed his head and prayed, "Heavenly Father, show your mercy and love to Ron." Then he quietly left.

"I followed the pastor to his car, apologizing," Heather continued. "He put his finger over my lips and said, 'Listen, you don't have to say a word. I know that Ron is a homosexual, and I can sense the misery you've endured. I wanted to warn you when you were planning your wedding. I had counseled him years before and promised never to reveal his secret. I felt I couldn't violate my counseling vows. Perhaps that was wrong. Maybe I should have told you. Certainly Ron should never have married you. I feel sympathy for him, but more so for you and your children. My advice to you is that you see an attorney and file for an annulment. He misrepresented himself to you, so you need not suffer through a divorce.' " The minister went on to tell her that her case was not an isolated one. "I am at present counseling 12 wives from our congregation whose husbands insist on oral stimulation or the act of oral sex. They are nervous, depressed and repulsed by having to oblige."

Heather loved Ron, and it took all of her courage to go to an attorney and file for an annulment. I agreed to be a witness for Heather.

When I met Heather at the courthouse the morning of the hearing she was clutching a red card in the palm of her right hand. She showed it to me: "The Lord Is My Defence" (Psalm 94:22) it read.

At the hearing Heather stood before the judge and told her story. The judge then asked for Ron to state his position. He stood up, said not a word and walked out the door. When Ron's attorney was called to the stand, he shook his head. "I have nothing to say."

The judge then ordered the court records sealed and granted the annulment.

When I sat down with Heather over lunch, there was no elation in her eyes. They were sad, reflective. "Betty, I feel the Lord has freed me from bondage, and I'm grateful. Nor do I feel anger and resentment toward Ron. He is still a prisoner. I wish there was some way he could be helped."

"I hope he seeks it," I replied.

"I do too. But if he wouldn't seek it to save our marriage, I don't think he will now. He'll go on living as a gay—maybe more openly."

"How can they call themselves 'gay' when their lives are so sad?" I asked.

Heather shook her head. "I don't feel judgment toward Ron. I just feel an overwhelming sense of my own sin. I distorted scripture. I took a passage and twisted it to get what I wanted. My prayer was wrong. God probably granted it to teach me a lesson."

"I don't think God would punish you for wanting a husband so much," I replied. "But I'm beginning to see that if we pray dangerous prayers, He may allow them to be answered."

Heather looked confused. "I thought God answered prayer or He didn't—yes or no. If He turns His back on the wrong kind of prayer, then how does it get answered?"

"Satan can answer prayers too. More people than you think pray to him."

Heather shivered. "I see what you mean. My prayer was so misguided that Satan picked it up and had a field day with me." She looked at me hard. "I want to go to church, Betty. I want to get down on my knees and ask God's forgiveness and repent of my actions. I want to be clean inside again."

Heather did get a cleansing. Her marriage to Ron was a costly experience, but I am praying that God will find a way to use it for good.

8

THE ANONYMOUS PRAYER

THERE ARE TIMES when prayers for certain types of needy people must be uttered without their knowledge. When some individuals hear of prayers being said for them, they become angry or sarcastic at those praying and at God and can thus nullify the effect. But a quiet, persistent prayer can have a strong healing effect on a difficult person if he or she doesn't know it is being said. I call these "anonymous prayers" because the author of them remains unknown.

The promise for this is in Matthew 6:6. "When you pray, go into your room, close the door and pray to your Father, who is unseen. Then your Father, who sees what is done in secret, will reward you" (NIV).

I liken the spreading impact of the anonymous prayer to the power of one kernel of corn. Given proper time and care, one kernel of corn, anonymously hidden in the dark earth, produces two stalks on which are usually found a yield of two cobs of corn each.

One day I examined several ears of yellow corn. I counted the rows. Every cob, I discovered, contains an even number of rows. There are more rows on a large cob, but nature is consistent and there are always an even number of rows. After counting the number of grains on all the ears, they averaged out to 716 grains each. Some yield from one kernel!

For one grain planted, you receive a harvest of approximately 2,856 grains in return.

I believe the chain reaction effect of prayer far exceeds the yield of one kernel of corn. And anyone making this investment of time and energy can have a fruitful ministry with people without their knowing of it. God won't bless it, of course, unless it is in line with His teachings and purpose.

Tell a person, "I am praying for you," and you may threaten him. But the anonymous prayer, being no threat, can do its work quietly.

It was effective with my mother's father, Dad Burns. Early in life he was turned off of religion by a weepy-voiced woman who dedicated her solo to him on the occasion of one of his rare appearances in church. She was completely sincere when she looked sadly at him and sang, "Will the Circle Be Unbroken By and By?" Dad Burns decided that, yes, this was one circle he would not be a part of.

My mother began praying for her father when she was in her teens. He was a contractor and had to climb heights in his building profession. She feared that someday he would have a fatal fall and was not prepared to enter Heaven.

Dad Burns was a family entertainer, and we children loved him. When the conversation would get controversial, or the kids squabbled, or a religious or political discussion would get out of hand, he had this "thing" he did. He would jump to his feet and, hopping about on one foot, pretend he was playing a violin rendering sweet music. He would sway and grimace like a great maestro, make-believe violin under his chin, bow plucking strings with virtuosity. We were all so doubled up by this act that the angry words died away in laughter.

On occasions when someone would talk to him about his eternal soul, he would pull this same violin scene. Once when Uncle Arch, his brother-in-law minister, talked seriously with him on this subject, Dad Burns grabbed his hip pocket and said, "This is my god," slapping his pouch of chewing tobacco.

Soon the anonymous prayer for Dad Burns spread from his wife and my mother to others in the family. Since he had placed chewing tobacco on the throne as his god, this habit became the target of their prayers.

As children, my four brothers and I would pretend we were Dad Burns. We carried raisins in our pockets, chewing and spitting, just like him. We almost worshiped the man with his gentle, comic, happy-go-lucky ways.

Dad Burns had an almost continuous dialogue with Uncle Arch. "I'd like to go to your Heaven, Arch, but you know they won't let me chew and spit on them golden streets up there. The first time I splatter tobacco juice on them golden streets, Saint Peter will kick my rear end right outta there. And if I can't take my tobacco with me, I ain't goin'. It and me; we've been buddies for 41 years now, and I'm not gonna stop." The adults would look pained, the children amused and Uncle Arch would change the subject.

When we girls started dating, Dad Burns promised that he would not chew and spit in front of our dates. He didn't either.

One day, I heard my mother tell my dad, "Glenn, I'm not going to worry about Dad anymore. I have prayed for him since I was a girl, but just recently I've had the assurance that it won't be too long now."

Nine years after that, on a Sunday night, he volunteered to go to church. At the close of the sermon, he got up, walked forward and knelt at the altar, weeping. He didn't merely accept Jesus, he implored Jesus to please accept him. No one had asked him. There had not been a formal appeal or plea or altar call. Later he told us, "The Spirit of God carried me up there and humbled me to my knees."

My grandmother called at 9:30 that night to tell us about it. "Dad laughed and cried and hugged and loved everyone who was there," she said. "I cannot tell you how changed he is. And energy! I've never seen him so on fire to get on with his new life."

Three days later our family went to visit them. When Dad

Burns came home for lunch he could hardly eat he was so eager to tell us of his new-found joy. "I feel as free and clean as a small child," he concluded.

"What about your tobacco?" Mother asked. "Is it still so important to you?"

A surprised look spread over his face. He slapped his hip pocket and yelled, "Tobacco?" Then he pulled out the pouch. It was flat as a pancake. "I'd plain forgot all about it," he said in amazement. It seemed he had been sliding around, working on a roof for three days, wearing the same pair of blue striped, bibbed overalls. No wonder his pouch of tobacco looked so battered.

"That's a miracle!" he exclaimed. He took out the pouch and put it in my grandmother's maple hutch cupboard where it would serve as a reminder that God did work miracles. The last time I looked, several years later, it was still there where he could point it out to young people when they told him they were hooked on a habit. "Let God do it for you," he would tell them.

Members of my family had been praying for Dad Burns for more than 18 years. That may seem a long wait for an answer to prayer like this, but it's God's timing, not ours, that matters. If we're faithful—and those who prayed anonymously did so month after month, year after year—He will always answer our prayers.

It was an old television series, "The Millionaire," which started me praying for unsuspecting people. In the television series a wealthy benefactor would give a million dollars to startled people with certain deep needs. How they handled this gift made good television drama.

I hadn't any money to give away, but a desire came to pray anonymously for people's needs, then watch with joy and delight as their problems were resolved.

The first time I saw this principle work in a miraculous way was with my brother, Jim. He and his wife, Bobbie, lived in a modest but cute house in Houston, Texas. They desperately wanted a family, but after seven years of marriage they were still childless. Tests showed that Jim's sperm count was too low for reproduction.

Just before Easter in 1965, my father, mother and I drove to Houston for a visit with Jim and Bobbie Perkins. After dinner that first night we were congratulating Jim on his financial and business success. "All that's fine," he replied, "but I'm a 200-pound failure when it comes to reproduction."

Later on that evening Mother caught my eye and motioned for me to follow her. We went into Jim and Bobbie's bedroom, and she shut the door behind us. "Betty, I want to do something. This will be our secret. I believe there is special power in the anonymous prayer we make for other people. And for two reasons. First, the person being prayed for isn't defensive and can't resist the prayer. Second, the person praying can't get conceited when the answer comes because the receiver of the answer doesn't know whom to thank but God, which is the way it should be."

We knelt beside their bed. I'll always remember this scene. The bedspread was of quilted satin in a mint green color; the entire room was decorated in pale lavender with accents of mint green and shades of olive. Mother carefully placed both hands on the bed. I did the same. Then Mother prayed, "Lord, as we two agree that it shall be done, we lay our hands on this bed, the place where Jim and Bobbie become one flesh, asking you to make it the scene of a glorious, happy and rewarding conception of a new life. Give them a child of their own to bring joy into their home. If it be Thy will, let the little one have soft, big, brown eyes like Jimmie."

She broke down for a few minutes, then gained control and went on. "We're going to expect it to happen, Lord, for nothing is impossible with You. You alone are the Maker of life. We trust You for everything."

Before we left the room, she made me promise her that this would be our secret prayer and that I would continue to pray it on my own until it came to pass.

Lisa Jeanette Perkins was born February 2, 1966, slightly more than 10 months after mother's and my anonymous prayer pact. She had big, soft, brown eyes like her daddy's.

With the birth of Lisa, Mother's and my prayer pact ended, and I was free to tell this story. I'm not sure I understand the power in this kind of secrecy, but I know it is something God honors. Holding a heartfelt desire under protective silence seems to give it power; talk about it too much and the power dissipates. The same principal applies to something important I feel impelled as an author to put down on paper. If I discuss it with too many people beforehand, the material gets diffused and loses impact.

The secrecy principle also applies to another area—thanksgiving. The word itself is made up of 12 letters, six for *thanks*, six for *giving*. Thanks is open gratitude and praise. Giving is the prayer-in-secret half of thanksgiving as advised by Jesus when He said: "When you give . . . do not let your left hand know what your right hand is doing, so that your alms (giving) may be in secret; and your Father who sees in secret will reward you" (Matthew 6:3–4, RSV).

When my father became the pastor of the little, red-brick church in Clinton, Indiana, he took one look at the small parsonage built right up against the church and realized that my four active brothers would be batting baseballs through the windows of that pretty little sanctuary. The manse was rented to a widow and my folks bought a place 11 miles south in the country with an orchard and where we could have a garden, pets and lots of space. We would also be far away from a certain local pool hall which had a bad reputation.

Ishmael Burgess owned this pool hall which drew all the undesirable characters of the area along with their unmentionable activities. One night I overheard my mother say to my father, "Moving away from that place of iniquity is fine for us, but what about people living nearby? Let's pray in faith that God will close that spot down." My father agreed, and I heard them talking quietly to God about that pool hall numerous times but never openly.

Ishmael's wife was named Verdie, a snappy woman with black hair, sharp, black eyes and a happy-go-lucky smile. She was active in our church, and everyone loved her. Becky Wallace and her husband were also active in the church. Becky was Ish's sister.

One night about midnight we were all aroused from sleep by a knock at our door. I crept out of bed and watched my father open the door to a man who could hardly stand up and whose speech was thick and almost incoherent.

"Reverend, hep me," the man said. He mumbled something I couldn't hear. Then the word "lost" came through.

"I'll drive you home, Ish," my father said. "You can return for your car tomorrow."

The owner of the pool hall pulled his head up and with red eyes and swimming head, looked straight at my dad, his speech suddenly quite clear. "You should know what I mean," he shouted. "I know the way home, but I'm still lost cause I don't know the way to God. I want peace like Verdie's got. And my sister Becky and her husband's got it too."

I edged closer as my parents invited him to sit down. I had never been this close to a drunk before. I was also concerned because Verdie, his wife, was one of my favorite people. At the invitation of my folks, Ish tried to kneel for prayer, but he slumped against the couch, again in a drunken heap.

Then Daddy spoke. "Lord, sober him up so that he knows what he is doing. Free him, Lord, from his misery. Give him Your peace of soul."

At this point Ish began to sob and pray. As he did so, he began to straighten up, and the words came through clearly as he talked seriously to God.

Then to my surprise he began to laugh with joy and astonishment that God had so instantly sobered him up. Soon he was carrying on a normal conversation with my parents.

He didn't need my dad to take him home, but Daddy dressed and drove our car, with Ish following in his. My father wanted to introduce Verdie to her new husband.

Ish not only became the only reformed drunk in town, he delighted most of the townspeople by closing down the pool hall and selling the building to a furniture store. And so my parents' secret prayer pact regarding the pool hall had a happy result, coming about in a somewhat surprising way. Ish spent the last 18 years of his life as a leading citizen. He died a few years ago. I feel I'm free now to tell about my parents' secret prayer about Ish.

I shared the anonymous prayer theory with a young man I'll call Walter, who approached me about a financial "sore" that was festering and infecting a friendship.

Walter had loaned a friend a sum of money to make a down payment on a house. His friend agreed to make payments of $50 each month to reimburse him for the loan by depositing it in the bank in Walter's savings account and was given deposit slips to do so.

Months passed. Walter went to the bank to withdraw money from his savings account and learned that the friend had not made one single payment. When he phoned his friend, he was always "out."

Walter mailed him regular monthly reminders, then wrote a letter saying to the friend, "I want your friendship even if you can't pay me right now. I will be patient and wait for the money. Please don't avoid me."

At this point, I shared with Walter some of my prayer experiences. He agreed to try it. He left his friend alone, did not tell anyone else about the situation nor that he was praying for the man.

One year later Walter's friend was transferred to another state into a new job. Walter wondered if that was the last he would ever see of his money and his friend.

Several months later a registered letter arrived addressed to Walter. Inside was a bank draft covering the entire loan, but not the agreed-upon interest of seven percent. Instead, he had increased it to 10 percent.

One morning I was walking through the doorway from my husband's study into the den. As I passed through the doorway, the words ran through my mind, "Sanctify yourselves, for tomorrow the Lord will do wonders among you." It was Saturday, and I tried to keep my mind on my housecleaning, but the words stayed in my head.

I found the passage in Joshua 3:5. *These words were spoken to Joshua, not to us,* I rationalized. But they continued to ring in my ears: *"Sanctify yourselves,"* came the emphatic word, "for tomorrow the Lord will do wonders among you." Both Carl and I walked around all that day filled with expectancy. It was a Saturday. Other Saturdays had not always been like this. Sometimes we quarreled on Saturday. The combination of April watching cartoons on television, the pressure on Carl to finish his sermon preparation, combined with the sounds of my organ music as the soloist came for rehearsal, all produced crackling tension in our home. As a result whenever pressure came to our household we said, "It must be Saturday."

When the words "sanctify yourselves" refused to die away, I stopped my cleaning and went into Carl's study. He listened and quickly decided that God was talking to me. "There's only one thing to do in a situation like this," he said. "When you know you should pray but don't know what for, then use Romans 8:26-27." He got out his Bible and read the words: "Likewise the Spirit also helpeth our infirmities: for we know not what we should pray for as we ought: but the Spirit itself maketh intercession for us . . . He that searcheth the hearts knoweth what is the mind of the Spirit, because He maketh intercession for the saints according to the will of God."

"Betty, you and I are Spirit-filled. Let's ask Him to use us." We did, together, praying as the Bible suggested, a slight variation of the anonymous prayer. Then we forgot about it until the next morning.

The Sunday morning church service went smoothly. Carl and I were saying good-by to parishioners when we noticed our dentist, John Eagle, and his wife, Cynthia, talking to some people who were sitting on the back pew of the sanctuary. John motioned for us to come over. Walking toward them, we found a most pathetic sight. A pale, anemic young woman in her 20s was sitting there holding on her lap a baby girl. Beside her was a frightened, older girl whom we quickly discovered was deaf.

The woman introduced herself as Dee Standish. Terribly ill with a bowel blockage for four days, suffering from a chronic kidney infection, weighing only 89 pounds, she said she had come to her grandmother's house in Houston to die. Her tests at the Charity Hospital the day before showed an obstruction, and blood tests pointed toward malignancy. Her anemia, low blood count and bladder infection history made surgery a very great but necessary risk. When her husband had deserted her, she had become a stripper to make a living for her two children.

Neither the mother or her children had ever been to church. Since the young woman was totally unprepared for the death she faced, her grandmother suggested they visit our church which was the nearest. The threesome had crept inside during the service.

"I don't really want to live," she told us, "but I do want help for these two, especially Darlene, who can't hear and won't talk." Looking at my husband she pleaded, "Will you pray for them?"

It tore at our hearts. We prayed together softly so as not to frighten the children; I do not remember my words, yet I'm completely certain that this prayer was anointed. I remembered then the words that God had given me the day before: "Sanctify yourselves for tomorrow the Lord will do wonders among you." This was tomorrow!

He would do the wonders! I would be His instrument. What an assurance!

Then followed the feeble, shaking voice of Dee. "God, forgive my awful sins, my body sins, my cursing mouth. Please give me strength to face surgery tomorrow morning."

Dee promised to have her grandmother call us when surgery was performed. We heard nothing from Dee or her grandmother until the next Wednesday night. As Carl and I were entering the church sanctuary for the midweek service, a well-dressed, rather young woman bounced through the double glass doors, grabbed my husband's elbow and began shaking his arm. "Don't you know me? I'm Dee. You won't believe this—or maybe you will."

We finally did recognize her as the girl with the terrible dilemma we had met on the back pew three days before. What a story she had to tell! When she entered the hospital that Sunday night, she was so much better it amazed the nurse who had viewed her records.

When they started prepping her for surgery the following morning, her blood count startled the surgeon. It had jumped from a life-threatening low to a normal red blood cell level. The test showed no more kidney infection and the obstruction was gone. They gave her an enema, and her bowels moved normally. Kept in the hospital two extra days, she regained strength so fast that they finally released her as cured. Her first stop after leaving the hospital was to our church for a joyous report.

Several days later, Dee called to tell us that the nine-year-old deaf child, Darlene, had just come running into the kitchen terribly excited. She had been watching television when suddenly she heard the voices. "I can hear, Mommy," she cried. "I can hear." Darlene is now in a special class, catching up rapidly on the three years of school she missed.

Dee is now so well and strong that she can't do enough for the sick. Talented in art and ceramics, she creates humorous cards and gifts to cheer convalescents. When April was thrown from a horse and broke her collar bone, Dee made a "Raggedy Ann" and "Raggedy Andy" for her. She brings her own art designs to the church for use at baby showers, wedding receptions and other special occasions. Regularly she visits the nursing home near where she lives, telling her story to cheer up the patients.

The Christmas after her miracle, I received a special letter from her. Here it is in part:

Dear Betty:

A few months ago, I looked forward to Christmas with fear and dread and did not expect to live to see it. My life changed that day I walked into church. God saw a tired, dying, stubborn girl who did not believe in Him. All I could do was cry because I was so scared. When I saw you and those other people crying tears for me, a nobody, a wasted life, a horrible sinner, I could not believe it. None of you knew me, and I did not know you.

When you put your arm around me and held my hand and prayed for me, I felt a shock go through my body. When I left that day, I knew God was with me. God is so wonderful! He healed me and restored my mind. I did not deserve it. Christmas looked sad, but now it is the best Christmas I ever had in my whole life.

I want to help others the way you people have helped me and the way God has helped me.

Sealed with a prayer for you,

Your friend,
Deana "Dee" Standish

There were not only occasions when we were to pray for certain people anonymously, but at times we would be asked to pray in the Spirit for situations only God knew about. My prayer education was continuing.

9

A MOVING ADVENTURE

AFTER THREE YEARS in Pasadena, Texas, I was seized with an unaccountable restlessness. What was wrong? Texas had been good to us; the people in our church were loving and supporting. Carl's ministry had been strong; the church had tripled in membership. My book, *My Glimpse of Eternity*, had become a surprise best seller, inundating me with a flood of requests for personal appearances.

All this indicated the Lord's blessing, and I was grateful. But the restlessness was still there.

Was I doing something wrong? No clear, single answer came out of my prayers. Obviously I was a flawed person in several ways, but this did not seem to be the basis for my unrest.

Meanwhile I found myself thinking often of my childhood back in rural Indiana. The apple orchard on Stop 18 Road, the creek bank at Mom Burns'; mossy, damp wood paths lined with wild violets, jack in the pulpit, dandelion, and mayapple plants. I yearned once again to pick wild greens with Mom Perkins, then wash them, cook them with a ham bone and eat them. I wanted to sit at a window with a view of a clear sky instead of freeways cluttered with thousands of cars.

Perhaps reading will fill the emptiness, I thought. I read *Country*

Chronicle, Wild Rivers and Mountain Trails, Locust Hill, Young Pioneers, I'll Take the Back Roads, Daughter of the Land, Wilderness Wife, and *Grandma's Attic.* My discontent only deepened. How I longed to trade in the exhaust fumes for a breath of unused, fresh, country breeze, for the smell of cow dung, or fresh mown hay in the loft of a red barn. I kept my feelings to myself. My husband is naturally restless, and I knew my feelings would trigger that restlessness. He was more satisfied than I had ever seen him. I determined to control my desires.

I went to an auction with Carl and April, and we bought an old school bell, a little black pot-bellied stove, an old wash board and a kerosene lamp. These would enable me to fix up our new, brick parsonage with some nostalgic antiques. I could be content in just pretending. This touch of nostalgia got to Carl, however, and he preached a refreshing sermon on "Back to the Basics":

> Back to the Bible;
> Back to the family altar;
> Back to the church as it was meant to be;
> Back to caring for people as individuals.

He used as a text, Jeremiah 6:16. ". . . look and ask for the ancient paths, where the good way is; and walk in it, and find rest for your souls" (RSV).

My married daughter, Brenda, wrote to tell us she was pregnant. "Bud and I want to have this baby the old fashioned way: natural childbirth," she said. "I have been learning to crochet. I already know how to knit so I can make so many pretty little things. Perhaps it is the old homing instinct, but I bought a bushel of apples to do some canning; I also want to make strawberry jam. All the married students here are canning and making homemade bread. One couple is using a wood stove. Some are doing nature farming and selling vegetables. I've learned to make candles. P.S. Bud said to tell you he's the one who made the bread. Also, I am going to breast-feed my baby, quit my teaching job in the music department of the elementary schools and be a real mother."

I wrote back to tell Brenda that I had bought an old galvanized tub like the one I took a bath in as a kid. Everyone seemed to be restoring old cars, old houses, old furniture and getting a new thrill out of old delights.

As I drove to the Houston airport to catch a plane to Norfolk, Virginia, for an appearance on the "700 Club," I was thinking about our long-legged collie dogs, cooped up in a chain link fence on a lot the size of a bedsheet. And the mare and the colt we had to drive four miles to visit and exercise. If only they were free to run without getting killed in the wild traffic. Then came a spontaneous prayer: "Lord, You must have a better place for us to live than this. If You do, please lead us to it."

While waiting to be interviewed on television by Pat Robertson, I heard the music of the Lowell Lundstrom Family. I remembered they were from South Dakota, and nostalgia overcame me again. How I had loved the four years Carl and I had spent at "Whispering Pines" in North Dakota.

During the station break, just before I was interviewed, I felt a hand tap my shoulder. It was Lowell Lundstrom himself: author, minister and head of the institute bearing his name. "Tell your husband to call me when you get home. I think I have a position that will interest him. We're about to go on weekly television. I desperately need someone to help me. Carl would be perfect. Please twist his arm. Tell him it's time to leave the big city and come back to the prairies."

He had no way of knowing how homesick this country gal was and how like music to my ears were those words. But I doubted if Carl felt the same way.

Carl surprised me. He was interested and agreed to pray about it. Could South Dakota be God's place for us?

To test the water I wrote a letter and addressed it to "Newspaper, Sisseton, South Dakota." In the letter I wrote: "Please send me your Sunday paper including the houses for sale advertising section." I enclosed a dollar.

A return note appeared in a few days: "Dear Mrs. Malz: One paper only, Thursday, once a week. I sent you one today. I don't think there are any houses for sale. Most people don't list them in the winter. Peggy"

I wrote back: "Dear Peggy: Please scout around and see if there are any old farm houses for sale. I'll pay you for your time." She wrote back: "You don't need to. Our population is 3,700. Everybody knows if anyone sells their place. I'll let you know if one is available."

One morning Carl emerged from his study and said, "You know, if I thought we could find another place like Whispering Pines, I wouldn't mind making this move. April has always wanted to enjoy snow. I do hate to see our youngest child grow up in a congested city."

He made a phone call, arranged for an interview, flew to Minneapolis where he met with Lowell Lundstrom and returned home with a new job.

I was thrilled, jubilant, awed. When the Lord moved, He moved!

We decided that a 1,700-mile move would have to be a major prayer project. But also a fun project. I had a sense of delicious expectancy that if we completely trusted God in all aspects of the move to South Dakota, He would give us joyful surprise after surprise.

We sat down with April and talked about all the things involved in a long-distance move. Then we made a list of things we wanted God to work out for the good of all concerned with our move:

> Find us a country home in South Dakota.
> Provide Carl's church in Texas with an excellent pastor.
> Provide the money we will need for the move.
> Help us find the right equipment including horse trailer and tow-bar.
> Help the animals not to get sick.
> Protect our car as we travel in it.
> Keep us healthy.
> Give us good weather for travel.

As I looked over the list, I thought to myself, "If only we could find a home by a lake." I put this in the form of a prayer, then thrust it aside as too much to ask. "You know what is best for us, Lord," I concluded.

Since we had only a modest sum for a down payment on a home, we placed a call to the bank in Sisseton, South Dakota. The bank president, Harold Torness, was most helpful and informed us there were two roomy houses available near my husband's work but not even one prospect of a country place. He explained that most farms in the area were passed down generation after generation within a family.

This was discouraging. We prayed again for a place where our animals would be free to roam and where Carl, April and I could be close to nature.

The following morning a call came from Mr. Torness. There was a house, 75 years old and terribly run down which might be available. The property contained 21 acres. He wasn't sure the owners wanted to sell, although they lived most of the year near McAllen, Texas. The house would take much remodeling, refurnishing and redecorating.

In the mail the next morning was an advertisement which grabbed my attention. It contained a picture of the tousled hair and head of Will Rogers, the famous country philosopher. Beside his photo was the quote, "Buy land. They ain't makin' any more of the stuff!"

I showed it to Carl. The message clicked with us. We would buy land, have a garden, have our own beef and pork. Regardless of how bad the house looked, those 21 acres beckoned.

Later the same day, Mr. Torness called. The owners were willing to sell at a price we could afford, but they could not vacate until May, four months off. This was perfect. April had to finish her school year. Carl told him, "We'll take it."

"Without seeing it?"

"Yes," Carl said. "We want a country place and if it is the only one available, it has to be the one God wants for us."

I'm sure the banker thought we were strange people. "I would not want to hold you to a deal like that. We'll just wait until you can come," he told Carl.

"Betty will come up in a couple of weeks to check it out," Carl replied after a short consultation with me. "In the meantime, we'll mail you a check for $1,000 as a deposit to hold it for us."

When I arrived the temperature had not been above zero for 62 days. Snow had stopped falling only an hour before I arrived and the temperature had managed to climb to 28 degrees above zero.

The roads were almost impassable, so I donned ski pants, heavy jacket with a hood and climbed on behind Mr. Torness for my first ride on a snowmobile. When we careened to a stop at the farmhouse, I fell out into a snow drift, dropping a camera, losing an earring and nearly losing one arm.

Brushing the snow from my eyes, I got a glimpse of many, many pine trees, the windbreak surrounding the whole property. Instantly I knew this was our home, another "Whispering Pines."

Mr. Torness had not told us it had two barns, a chicken house, a garage, an old one-room schoolhouse, and the original log cabin facing the creekbed where the owners had homesteaded when the Dakota territory was opened up 100 years ago. I loved everything about it: the trees, the broad expanse of sky, the view of Sisseton from the front windows, the panorama of orchard and hills on the south, the ski slope and woods on the north, the lane, the lilac hedge that would bloom in the spring, the grapevines—rows of them—that would provide fruit for our jellies.

"You may want to tear the old house down and build a new one," Mr. Torness suggested.

I shook my head vehemently. I had already lived in four new houses and soon grew to dislike every one of them. This would be our haven. I knew my husband would love it, and April could toboggan up and down the hills on our own property. For me it would be an especially good place to write. I was pleased to learn there were two springs on the property that furnished the drinking water. I had tired of chlorine and other "purifiers."

My eyes took pictures of the stairway and the upstairs bedrooms and one cozy little room for my writing studio that overlooked the orchard, the creek and the outbuildings. Before the move, I would have to find in Houston the wallpaper, fabrics and other things I needed to cheer up our country nest. The only thing it lacked to make it the Garden of Eden was a lake nearby. That would have been too much. Contended, I flew back to Houston.

The movers came, inventoried our furnishings and gave us May 1 as moving day. Their estimate was $2,300 which meant we would have to sell Carl's little, red, ragtop Volkswagen. This was a blow to Carl. His little "bug" got him smoothly in and out of freeway traffic and into small parking spaces, but we were leaving the city and the warm weather. The prairie farmers of South Dakota, who are used to two seasons—July and winter—would be amused if we arrived there driving a midget of a car. The cold wind would drift a bank of snow higher than a little car in one night.

Carl recalled the day he had financed his little car at the bank. One of the secretaries there had teased him, "If that car is ever missing you will know I've stolen it." He went to see her, and she still wanted it. Downstairs she went to the loan department and financed it on the spot. One more prayer had been answered.

We needed an economical, sturdy vehicle to pull a horse trailer with our mare and two-week-old colt. Larry Harvard, who lived around the corner from us, had been touting his Dodge Ramcharger. Carl walked over to him one day to get information.

"Why not buy this one?" Larry asked. "I'm washing it now so that I can put this sign up." He held up a placard: "For Sale." Only that day had he decided to sell it and buy an open-bed truck. Once again we saw how God's timing could meet our needs.

That night at dinner when Carl said grace he thanked the Lord for another answer to prayer. Then he said: "I'm taking a sizeable cut in salary to accept this job, Lord. But I feel You want me to take it. We're trusting You to help us manage it, to keep us healthy and to cut our expenses so that we can serve You with a relaxed mind and pleasant home atmosphere."

When he had finished April said, "Don't worry about me, Daddy. For years I've wanted to ride a school bus instead of walking. It's more fun to sit and talk with friends. Now we'll live four miles from town, and I'll be making new friends on a school bus. God knew what I wanted."

The week before our departure, my first royalty check arrived from the publication of my first book. It was $18 more than the salary cut Carl would be taking for the coming year. Sometimes God pays us in advance.

When I called the rental truck offices to try to rent a horse trailer, I learned the bad news. They no longer stocked them. I priced the new ones at a dealer. The cheapest was $1,600. There was a used one badly in need of repair for $600. But would it get us to South Dakota? I doubted it.

Once again we were dependent on prayer. "Lord, these animals are important to us. Now we have a real home for them in South Dakota. Please show us how to get them there."

The way He did was so amazing!

I was about to take our dog to the vet for her shot when the phone rang. It was the foreman at a nearby plant. "Mrs. Malz, I heard that you need to borrow a horse trailer. I have a new man here who just moved from Aberdeen, South Dakota. He might be able to help you."

There was a short silence then another voice came on. "My name is Eldon Bessler. I hear you need a horse trailer to transport your animals to South Dakota. We used one to move some of our furniture down here. We're going back to South Dakota in June to bring back our horses and dread the thought of pulling an empty trailer back up there."

Excitedly I told him we would take good care of it and
pay him as well.

"Let me talk to my wife about it," he said uncertainly.
"It may be too complicated to work out."

I gave him our address and hung up, wondering how I
might persuade Mr. Bessler of our reliability.

While he gave our collie her shot, I told the veterinarian
about our farm in South Dakota.

A young woman entered from the lab. "I want you to meet
my new assistant," the vet said. "She just started yesterday.
Cathy, this is Mrs. Malz."

We shook hands. "I heard you mention South Dakota.
That's where I'm from," Cathy said.

"That's strange," I murmured. "I talked to a man today
who is from South Dakota. He's new here too. I should get
you two together."

She thanked me and said she would like that because she
and her husband were homesick already.

The phone rang later that night. "This is Eldon Bessler
again. My wife met you at the vet's today. She says you're
all right. You can use our trailer for free. You're doing us
a favor. It's expensive to drag one that far. Pick it up when
you're ready to go, and we'll work out the details."

A coincidence, most will say. Call it what you will, but I
know that God is at work in all things. When you move "in
God," He moves in your behalf.

Still we were becoming concerned about expenses. The
charge of $2,300 for the moving van, driving two cars with
double gasoline expense, meals, motels—it all mounted up.

My car is an old MGA. I thought it would be wise to sell
it instead of moving it, until Carl pointed out that it gets
37 miles per gallon of gasoline. With energy problems ahead
we would really need it. Then another problem arose. We
had a trailer hitch on the Dodge Ramcharger to pull the
horse trailer but learned that it was impossible to find a tow-
bar to go behind our Oldsmobile that would fit a 1962 MGA.
What would we do? We were going to fill the MGA with

all our palms, banana trees and plants, and Carl would pull it behind the Olds. Calls to dealers were unproductive. Someone suggested that I get a welder to make one. Time was too short, I was told by one metal shop.

As I was leaving the shop office, I passed a lady coming in. On the drive back to the house, I prayed, "Lord, where is there a tow-bar to fit my car? You know all things. Please help us find one."

The phone was ringing when I came in the door. It was the lady who had pushed open the door as I was leaving the shop. She had stopped there to find out who owned my MGA. She had one just like it. You guessed it. She also happened to have a tow-bar and was willing to loan it to us for the trip, provided we would return it by rail freight. Nor would she accept pay for the use of it.

We had one more river to cross. The church board had received many applications for Carl's pastorate, but they were having trouble knowing how to find the right man. One morning after April left for school, Carl and I sat together across the table, he laid his hand on mine, and we prayed, "Lord, we cannot leave here until we feel that our people have chosen a man they are happy with. Help us, please."

I was driving home from feeding our two horses later that day. I needed one article at the grocery store—a head of cabbage for dinner. Inside the supermarket I noticed the special of the day: four packages of carrots for a dollar. I never look at the labels which show where vegetables are grown, but this time I did. On this bag it read, "Grown in Apopka, Florida."

A light went on inside me. Why was Apopka significant? Of course, Gary Chapin, the pastor who had ministered to me so lovingly when John died, now had a church in Apopka, Florida. He was the one who delivered the sermon on self-pity that had brought me out of my depression after that gloomy night when I sat in a cold tub of water so long.

I hurried home to talk to Carl. Would not Gary be perfect for this growing church amid this burgeoning community?

Carl agreed. Gary Chapin was enthusiastic, an inspired speaker, had a sweet gentle wife and a young family. He had a "drive" that never tired, and his motto was always "to give more." These people would love him, and I had a feeling he would love Texas.

Carl could only shake his head in awe. No wonder the board couldn't find the right man. It was Gary. We were the instruments He had to use.

Carl presented Gary's name to the board. The board asked Gary to come and candidate. He was their choice. Gary accepted. The people love the whole Chapin family, and the church and congregation are growing and moving forward.

What an adventure life becomes when you trust the Lord.

Moving day. The mare had not traveled in a horse trailer for two years and the colt, never. We had a tumultous struggle to get them inside. We agreed that Carl should stay, watch the moving van being loaded and finish up business matters. He would then drive the Oldsmobile, pulling the loaded MGA behind it. April and I started out first, driving the Ramcharger which hauled the horse trailer. The two dogs and cat went with us in the Ramcharger.

Four days to drive 1,700 miles may seem slow traveling, but we had no choice. Rest stops were needed every three hours for the animals, mainly the mare and the colt.

April and I began and ended each day with prayer. We asked God to help us find farms on the highway with clean barns for each of the four nights. Late in the day at just the right time He led us to a place of friendly, hospitable people. At every opportunity we got out and loved our animals, nuzzled them, crooned to them, talked to them, and they responded beautifully.

Our "zoo" arrived at the South Dakota farm at dusk, the sun just setting behind some distant hills. One by one each member disembarked, carefully tested the ground, then did a bit of a dance on the lush brown dirt. We had made it without mishap! *Thank You, Lord.*

But there was no food, no beds, no furniture, only the blankets in the car to sleep on. All the animals had to be put in the garage since there was no fence around the barn. Then a neighbor, Connie Brewster, arrived with some warm cookies. What a lift! This was going to be a wonderful home.

The next morning all of us—including the animals—ran around like a bunch of nuts, staring at the beauty of the countryside. There were wild flowers, tall trees, fruit trees and lush farm land. The only thing we didn't have was a lake. The nearest one was 13 miles away.

Carl arrived 26 hours after us. Then began the work of making a home out of a very old place. Three weeks passed. We had been too busy to get to know very many of our neighbors. The furniture had arrived and been put in place. I had wallpapered four rooms in five days while Carl put up the fences. There was painting to do every spare moment.

Amid the confusion something aggravated us. We heard heavy equipment roaring all day on our property line. I took one look and was distressed to find bulldozers clearing a nearby area. Was it to subdivide the land for a housing development? Carl was disappointed. "We might as well have bought a place in town if the town is coming to us," he grumbled.

One afternoon shortly thereafter a car drove onto our land, past the lilac hedge, by our orchard and up to our back door. Out stepped a good-looking couple with two children, a boy and a girl. They introduced themselves as our next door neighbors, Dr. Fred and Sandra Anderson; children: Rick and Kimber.

"Please come with us," Fred urged. "You've got to see something very special."

We looked so bewildered that the Andersons laughed. "You've been too busy to see what's been happening next to you. It is simply beautiful."

We followed them outside, got in their car and drove only a few yards when we saw it. Next to our property was a sparkling, beautiful new lake!

The Andersons had engaged the heavy equipment to construct a dam where two streams merged, forming a lake covering a six-acre area, 18 feet deep in the middle.

"The 500 trout we ordered will be here this week," Fred said proudly.

Our heads were spinning. As the sun went down, we saw the dogwood and redbud blossoms reflected in the reddish glow of the sun's reflection on the water. The willows framed the picture. What a breath-taking sight! Our hearts sang when we heard the generous words of our newly found friends and neighbors, "It's certainly big enough for us both. Use it, enjoy it."

As I mused over this tremendous new development, a verse was etched on my mind: "Delight thyself also in the Lord; and He shall give thee the desires of thine heart" (Psalms 37:4).

10

DIALOGUE WITH GOD

MY ADVENTURE WITH prayer was now in its 14th year. Six years of it had been spent "praying in" my husband. Then came the four-year period of family adjustment while Carl was at Trinity College in North Dakota. The turning point there was our discovery that our prayer focus should be on the needs of others. The result, to our surprise, was that it brought more meaning and fulfillment to us. And it prepared us for the three years of ministry that followed in Texas.

During this 14-year period came discoveries about prayers for God's guidance, how the Lord is in the minor events of life as well as the major, the impact of the one-word prayer—Jesus—the need to be careful about certain dangerous prayers and the extra power that comes through anonymous or secret prayers.

Inherent in all praying, of course, is dialogue: a two-way conversation. I discovered that generally I talked too much, listened too seldom, forgetting that half of the conversation belongs to the other person. Since I did this with people, I did it with God in prayer. I felt indicted by the misuse of my tongue.

So it was that I began to seek the advice of people less and less and go more and more to the greatest Source of wisdom.

"God, I am weak and unknowledgeable. If You still talk to people today, please talk to me."

Thus began a daily routine. Each morning when the alarm goes off at 6:20, I reach over and push in the alarm button. Then before I open my eyes, or turn back the sheet to even think about getting up, I pray, "Lord, I thank You for life and for this fresh, new morning. Give me strength and health for today. Help me to meet the people I'm supposed to meet and hear from those You want me to communicate with. Show me how to help them; or let me know if I am to receive something they have to give. Enable me to be a help and blessing to my husband and children today. Amen."

Then I pick up a clipboard beside my bed and wait to hear what He wants to say to me. God knows I will meet Him every morning so He has never failed to keep His appointment with me. I always feel His warm strength right then. The thoughts that come are my "marching orders" for the day.

At 7:45 A.M. comes our family appointment with the Lord. We have all had breakfast, and April is sitting at the table waiting for the school bus to arrive. She reads a short devotional in a booklet, "Our Daily Bread." Then Carl or I will say a short prayer: "Lord, help April to be an eager student, a good learner. Protect her from illness. When she is tempted to do wrong, give her *Your* power to refuse that temptation, to say no. May she be a good friend to other students, cooperative with her teachers and be one to encourage any who are depressed."

After the school bus has come and gone, I have a third appointment with the Lord. This is when I dialogue in depth with Him on our current needs and the needs of others. I have with me a list of items for prayer that I have collected during the past 24 hours; after presenting my petitions, again I linger and wait with a clipboard on my lap, writing down the things that I feel God is giving to me. I "go with the flow," feeling an enthusiastic eagerness about this time, for He has met me again.

The "knowing" that He is near me, talking to me, is not an eerie feeling. He is quiet-spoken, gentle, considerate; yet there is no softness but a steel-like quality to His words. They are not always what I want to hear; sometimes I am corrected for wrong thoughts and actions.

The Bible says, "Pray without ceasing." I try to do this in the form of a running dialogue with Him throughout the rest of the day. Why not? He is our dearest Friend, and we don't hesitate to carry on running conversations with friends while shopping, playing tennis or eating.

My talk with Him may begin at the sink as I do the breakfast dishes; it continues as I drive to town on some errands. The conversation is suspended during my work on a manuscript, but every now and then I stop and ask Him for the right word or thank Him for a new thought. I seek His counsel before an important telephone call or as I knock on the door of a friend I'm about to visit.

If I'm light-hearted, I will thank God for His many blessings; if I'm down, I tend to complain a bit. If I'm upset, I'll ask for special help. Always I try to be open and honest. I sense He hates phoniness worse than anything.

I have three clipboards in my house. I put one on my desk, one by my bed and one on the kitchen cabinet between the stove and the refrigerator. Many times I suddenly wake up in the night for no obvious reason. At first I would be somewhat annoyed at the interruption of deep sleep or a pleasant dream. Then I became aware that these could be God's nudges. If He is awakening me, then He wants my attention. That's the reason I put the clipboard beside my bed. Over the years I have received many valuable insights in the middle of the night. Some are used in books, or articles I write for magazines, or in letters to people with special problems. Some I have filed away for future use.

My mother called this the "rainbarrel method." When I was growing up, mother would never use the hard tap-water to wash my long hair. Instead, we had a rain barrel at the corner of the house and whenever it started to rain, she took off the lid of the barrel to catch as much of the soft rain as possible. (This is the listening part.)

After the rain, she put the lid on the barrel so the rain water would not become polluted. (This is the storing away of God's messages.)

Then, when my hair needed to be washed or a soft article of clothing needed sponging out, she already had her supply of good water. (This is the use of God's Word in a practical way to help someone else.)

Generally I sleep soundly for nine hours every night. When God awakens me, it is often because I have gotten too busy to talk to and listen to Him. He awakens me in different ways. Sometimes I think I hear a knock on the door and awaken. But there is no one knocking. God is knocking at the door of my heart. At other times I awake, thinking I heard the phone ringing. When I pick up the receiver, no one is at the other end. Occasionally, I hear Brenda's voice saying, "Mother." But Brenda lives a thousand miles away in Missouri. Once again it is the Lord getting my attention by using familiar things to alert me. No one else in the family hears these "sounds," so clearly they are internal nudges only.

One night I awakened, thinking I heard the phone. I waited. There was deep silence in the house. Then I felt His presence. I did not hear a voice, but I sensed He was reminding me of something. I turned on the soft light by my bed and reached for the clipboard and a pencil.

Then I wrote down one word: "Marcia."

Annoyed, I turned off the light and tried to go back to sleep. I didn't want to think about Marcia. The whole nasty situation surrounding her had happened eight years before.

But God wouldn't let me brush it off. "You owe her an apology," came the message.

I flared, "She owes me one, too."

The thought then came, "What I did for you, you can do for Marcia."

It was a sharp reprimand, and I was convicted. But I ducked doing anything about it.

The episode with Marcia occurred in the period before I met Carl. Marcia had a beautiful soprano voice. I often accompanied her on the piano or organ when she sang at clubs, luncheons and in churches. She confided in me one day that she had a crush on a young man with whom she worked.

I was suddenly furious with her. She had a fine husband, four children and a lovely home. How ungrateful! My husband, John, had died less than a year before, and I was living alone, discovering how few eligible, single men there were. One of the few such men was this person she was infatuated with! He was also a man I wanted to date.

I told Marcia I would never reveal her secret, but my sympathy shifted from her to her husband. I read portions in the Bible to her, showing how she was bordering on temptation's dangerous territory. I prayed with her, and she became overcome with guilt.

Her husband called me one day from work. "Betty I have to be out of town today. Will you go and see Marcia? Don't tell her I called you. She's so ill and depressed. She has confidence in you, and I feel you can draw her out and find out what's eating at her."

I promised to go and did. But I don't think I was helpful.

A few nights later I had a date with this young man Marcia was so smitten with. He was troubled. Marcia had confessed her love for him and had stated she would leave her four children and husband if he would run away with her. He wanted no part of it—or her. He asked me what he should do.

I told him to bow out. He agreed to stop seeing her.

When Marcia discovered her "crush" was dating me after rejecting her, she was furious. Our relationship was not only severed, she started rumors about my immoral relationships with men—all of them lies.

When Marcia's husband called me one day for advice, I felt God putting a restraining finger to my lips. The Lord also brought to my mind one of my dad's favorite quotes: "Suffer without complaining; be misunderstood without explaining."

But I disobeyed God's prompting and said these blunt words to Marcia's husband: "If I were you, I'd jerk Marcia off that singing job and fast. Men find her most attractive. Don't ask me any questions."

I knew I had done wrong the minute the words were out of my mouth. He did force Marcia to quit her job, and Marcia hated me from then on.

Years passed. Every time I heard a minister preach a sermon on restitution, I'd feel a sense of guilt and would reason with God something like this: "Marcia lied about me."

"You are to forgive her."

"But she wanted to do an immoral thing."

"That's not for you to judge. This is a problem she has with Me."

"But I haven't seen her for years."

"You can find a way. Remember, I gave you back your life. You have received much, so I expect much from you."

When I felt this reprimand I tried to rationalize. "Lord, she lives 1,700 miles from here. If I'm ever near her home, I'll go to her and ask forgiveness."

There was silence and I thought I felt a release. Maybe God only wanted to find out if I was just *willing*, in my heart, to be reconciled with Marcia.

But a low period followed when God seemed distant. I was floundering spiritually. Carl, April and I then took a vacation trip 1,100 miles from home. We stopped one evening at a smorgasbord restaurant which served cafeteria style. While standing in a long serving line, I turned around and gasped.

Marcia and her husband stood near the end of the same line.

I turned quickly in the other direction. They had not seen me. Since the line was so long and there were four different dining areas we might escape their detection.

Then came one of those firm inner thoughts, "Now is the time."

No more ducking or procrastination, He was saying, not if I wanted to have a continuing relationship with Him.

I whispered to April, "Tell Daddy I'm going to the ladies' room." There I studied my face in the mirror, took several deep breaths and asked God for the right attitude and the right words.

When I walked back and stood before them, Marcia was more shocked than I had been. I did not say a word, not even hello. I simply threw my arms around her.

"Forgive me," she whispered, tears in her eyes.

"Forgive me," I replied.

It was so quick, so quiet, yet so complete. To her husband it was a warm greeting of two old friends.

I introduced Carl to them, and we all sat together talking about the "wild coincidence" of our meeting. Marcia and I knew better.

During the months that followed came a long string of wonderful answers to prayer for Carl and me. The key to this, I'm convinced, was an act of forgiveness which came about because I was willing, first, to have regular dialogue with God, and second, to obey the directions He gave me.

Most mornings when I awake I have many burdens to share with the Lord, petitions to make. But there are times when I just feel adventuresome.

Closing my eyes, I then ask, "Lord, lead me to someone that I can give something to." When I pray this way I imagine there is a large, blank television screen before me. Then I wait for the Lord to flash a face on that screen.

One morning I had just done this when I saw on the screen the face of Doris Ferrend, a young woman who had been a neighbor when we lived in Terre Haute back in 1961. I hadn't seen her since.

Following this nudge, I wrote Doris a note and sent it to her old address. The letter was forwarded to her new home.

When Doris wrote back saying she now had three children and was battling cancer, I began praying for her. Then I learned from a friend that a new drug for cancer, thymidine, had just been used by a prominent local physician. Quickly I passed this information on to Doris and her doctor.

What was the result? I don't know. My role was to be obedient, to be a catalyst in such a situation. The results are up to Him. I do know that if I seek dialogue with Him, I have to follow through on His suggestions, no matter how strange they may seem to me.

Sometimes when we seek a dialogue with the Lord, He doesn't answer right away but later through a dream. It happened this way with our friend, Ted, who for two years had suffered with leg cramps and a toothache in one side of his mouth. An oral surgeon did tests and found nothing. Aspirin didn't stop the dull, aggravating ache that kept him from sleeping and eating.

One night Ted cried out in agony, "Oh God, tell me what the trouble is. If you can't tell me, speak to someone else who can."

No answer came and Ted fell asleep. He dreamed that he was walking into the kitchen and opening the refrigerator door. There was just one item inside—a red, one-half gallon carton of milk.

When Ted awakened, all he could think of was that red carton of milk. He went downstairs and drank a glass of milk, then went back to bed and slept well.

The next morning he wanted milk again. Ted continued to drink lots of milk, a half gallon a day. "I must be crazy," he thought. "Why should I need milk at age 29?"

He didn't say anything about it to anyone but continued drinking large quantities of milk for weeks. Then one day he realized that the leg cramps were completely gone, and his teeth had stopped aching.

An investigation by a bone specialist turned up the revealing facts. His mother had been terribly nauseated while carrying Ted and could keep little on her stomach. Extremely poor, his mother could not breast-feed him, nor was there money for enough milk. As a result Ted had a calcium deficiency.

God knew the problem, of course, and gave the answer to Ted when he asked for it.

God does not force His will on us, but when we do not follow His guidance, things usually go wrong in our lives. In late summer of 1978 I received an invitation from Westinghouse to do a television tour of five appearances in five cities in early November. I was physically tired from making the long move from Texas and from working so hard to redecorate the old house before cold weather came.

In the little room which is my writing studio, I knelt and prayed, "Lord, tell me whether I should do these television shows." There was no immediate answer, no thought planted in my mind, but I did feel a slight apprehension. Then the message came that God would talk to me from His Word. I was led to the 23rd Psalm and the phrase, "He restoreth my soul." As I read these words I felt His loving tenderness. He knew that I was weary and needed to be restored in my body, my mind, my spirit, my disposition.

I shut my eyes and saw a grocery store, empty but for one stock boy way in the back. In the quiet hours when there was no traffic, no people, and no business going on, this boy was restocking the shelves of that store. God impressed me with my need to be in the South Dakota wilderness so He could restock my shelves with new ideas and new vitality. I decided to refuse the television invitation.

But a close friend whose opinions I respected thought I should do it. "Television is great exposure. It will promote your book in a big way. We'll all be so proud of you."

Vanity and materialism won out. I accepted.

When I arrived in Pittsburgh for the first appearance I had a sore throat, and my voice was gravelly. I felt pressured by time in telling my story on the air and did not do a good job.

Back in my motel room, I lay on my bed and talked to God, "Lord, I've made a mistake. My throat hurts. I'm tense and irritable. The real person is not coming through."

I lay quietly, waiting. He was understanding. "I'm glad you've admitted your poor judgment. If a person repents, I can always redeem a mistake and bring good out of it."

In Philadelphia my voice quit twice and I had to drink water during the interview to keep going. Outside, I wrestled with four pieces of luggage getting in and out of cabs. No driver offered to help me.

In Boston I was weakened by cramps and diarrhea. On the flight to Baltimore my ears stopped up and stayed stopped up the remainder of the trip. From then on I had the feeling I was under water.

In the Baltimore motel room I flopped on the bed and whispered, "Lord, help me. They don't have a house doctor in the motel and I think I need one. What can I do?"

An hour later the phone rang. Friends from Texas visiting in the area had heard I was to be on television and had tracked me down. They hardly recognized my voice, I was so hoarse. They drove me to the emergency room of Mercy Hospital where I was treated for both a sore throat and a serious ear infection.

In San Francisco, I ran out of money, couldn't cash a check and went on a starvation diet the last two days. Wheezing and coughing I got on a plane from San Francisco to Minneapolis where we landed in a blizzard. My connecting flight was canceled, and I had to stay all night in a motel and charge the bill instead of coming home.

Meanwhile, Carl was due to leave the day after I got home for Charlotte, North Carolina, where he was scheduled to speak for 10 days at a marriage seminar. Sick, lonely, exhausted, I arrived home a day late and five hours after my husband had left on his trip. Sorrowfully I dragged myself home and into bed. God had warned me in advance not to take this trip. He knew how rough it would be and wanted to spare me. He did use me to witness to people on television, bringing some good out of a bad situation. But it took me weeks to recuperate.

The main purpose of a prayer dialogue is to hear what the Lord wants us to do. If we don't obey His instructions, it all goes for naught.

I'm learning that God never disputes His own Word when He speaks to men today. A linguist and book translator felt he had received word from God that he was to go overseas as a missionary. His wife refused to take him seriously because they had eight children to care for.

The linguist then reported to my husband that he heard God say He would send him a new mate to go with him to the mission field. My husband pointed out to the scholar that this could not be valid. God would not violate His commandments about the sanctity of marriage.

The linguist was obviously trying to find some reason for leaving his wife and family and was hearing the voice of his own desires.

While my dialogues with God have produced some great adventures in faith, I feel I've barely made a start in this form of communication. The messages received have often been fragmentary and puzzling and then again concise and hard-hitting. Sometimes I feel His presence, sometimes not. The enormity of a truth He gives me can be thrilling or chilling.

Always I want more. More of His love; more of His tenderness; more of His words; more of His reassurance. I strain always for more of Him, but then will resist making certain sacrifices to give myself more time to be with Him. What a paradox!

Sometimes I wish I would lose my sight for just a week— then get it back, of course, as good as before. It's when my eyes are closed that my deepest feelings occur. When I want to express myself most profoundly through music, I close my eyes. When my husband holds and kisses me, I feel his love more if I close my eyes. When I want to listen intently to an orchestra, I close my eyes to be able to sort out individual instrumentation and softer tone qualities that are not registered in the overall flow of sound.

I believe that when a person is blind, the sensitivity and concentration that would have been spent on seeing and taking eye pictures is focused inward and divided between listening and feeling. The sensitivity and understanding of the blind for the feelings of others amazes me. Many feel that God has smiled on them in their sightlessness. They are not distracted by the appearances of people and objects about them; they can focus on the true, internal, spiritual quality of others. Their ability to listen to the voice of God in prayer dialogue gives them an extra dimensional ability to help others without being discouraged or disconcerted by a facial expression of doubt, disinterest or unbelief.

Four mornings after the funeral of my young husband, John, the phone rang. My world was bleak; I was several months away from giving birth to April.

"Betty, my name is Horace Booker. I just learned of your husband's death and was concerned about your facing child-birth alone without him. My wife Julia is the one giving your daughter, Brenda, piano lessons. This morning we prayed that God will strengthen you and give you His joy since you have been robbed of yours. I believe the Lord spoke a mes-sage for me to give to you. Read the 54th chapter of Isaiah. It was written for the widow."

I followed his instructions and read the chapter prayerfully. It was comforting and reassuring. I was also fascinated by Horace Booker's insight and concern for others because I knew he had been born blind.

He called again, and I asked him for details about himself.

"God first started talking to me when I was a child," he replied. "Being blind and small in size I was alone and inside when the other children were out developing skills in sports and other activities. The Lord told me that He had chosen me for special work. He gave me a love for music and the extra time to develop this talent to inspire others. I never had to worry about dust or disorder or the arrangement of the house or the appearance of people. I just concerned myself with the love atmosphere of the house, filling it with music and caring."

Horace Booker then went on to describe an encounter he had with the Lord one day. "Lord, I need someone to love and someone who will love me just as I am," Horace said. "And Lord, if it be Your will, let my mate be able to see, to be my eyes for me and to drive a car to take me to churches where I play sacred concerts."

Horace explained that God did not answer in words but with an outpouring of understanding and assurance. It was palpable. God was going to act.

"At the very next concert a young woman named Julia came to hear me play." Horace went on. "Afterwards she came up and spoke to me. The first words were hardly out of her mouth before I knew she was the one."

Horace described their courtship, marriage and how perfectly their lives meshed. She drove for him, and they played sacred concerts together, Horace on organ, Julia on piano. They became lovers and teammates.

"Julia is so lovely," he continued. "I don't deserve her. I've touched her face, traced her features, and discovered that everything about her is beautiful."

Horace was so eloquent about his wife it brought tears to my eyes. Julia is sweet, gentle, even tempered, kind and never critical; she is also a large woman with plain features. "Man looketh on the outward appearance," says Scripture, "but the Lord looketh on the heart" (1 Samuel 16:7). So do blind men who love.

Because Julia's work kept her away during the day, Horace found he had some free time. He had another dialogue with the Lord, praying, "I need something to do now at home. I'm not too old to start a new career, Lord. Show me what You want me to do."

The answer came, "Have Julia read to you each day the list of deaths in the obituary column of the newspaper. You record them on tape. Then find an information operator who will help you get the telephone numbers of the survivors. Call them and comfort them. When they realize that you too have a handicap, it will help them to count their blessings."

Horace then explained that this was how he happened to call me. He "read" of my husband's death in the obituary column. "Sometimes I play and sing for these grief-stricken people," he said. "The calls keep me very busy because with most of the population being elderly here in Florida, there are so many deaths. I hope I've helped you, Betty. You may be sure I'll pray for you every day. Someday I'll see you and the others I've called. The two people I want to see more than anyone are my Julia and the face of my Jesus. These two have truly loved me and cared for me."

Here is a sum-up of my discoveries so far about conversational prayer:

1. God expects it, wants it from His children.

2. It's best done alone with Him. It can take place throughout daily activities. Preferably both. It should have the highest priority.

3. Listening means silence. A sense of expectancy. Patience. Some answers are a long time coming.

4. God speaks in different ways: a thought dropped on the mind, gentle words flowing through the Spirit, a sharp prodding in the emotions. He may speak through a dream. Very seldom do we hear an actual voice.

5. If we seek Him in dialogue, we must obey His instructions.

6. If we hear something that seems to be from God but we're not sure, we should test it through Scripture and the counsel of Godly people we trust.

11

PRAYER
FOR THE RESISTANT

SHOULD I PRAY for people who want no part of God? Is this an intrusion? Is such prayer effective, or a waste of time and breath?

When these questions arose, the answers I received from Christians and from Scripture were: "Yes, pray for nonbelievers. This is very scriptural. God wants His followers to reach every person in the world with His message of hope and salvation."

I accepted these answers, but the words were not real to me until I became involved with Betty and Roy Miller. The transformation of this couple and their children, largely through the prayers of concerned people, is an amazing story. It taught me that the rescue of lost, miserable and pagan persons can depend on a chain of praying believers, and that as a link in that chain I dare not be weak or absent when my time of responsibility comes.

Back in the 1960s, Betty, a lonely divorcee with two small sons, slipped off by herself one night to the lounge of a cocktail bar in Green Bay, Wisconsin. She was a petite, striking brunette, with warm brown eyes and a lithe grace that made her a superb ballroom dancer. Betty was sitting alone at the bar when she met Roy Miller.

Roy, a father with two daughters, was also lonely and full

of self-pity. His marriage was going sour. Roy was dark-haired, handsome, smooth-talking.

Betty and Roy met several more times, fell in love and decided to get married. Parents on both sides expressed strong disapproval. Betty was a Roman Catholic, Roy a Lutheran. Roy's father was a clergyman.

The confrontation between father and son was an angry one and went something like this: "I intend to get a divorce and marry Betty." Roy said bluntly.

"It's wrong in every way," replied his father. "You are responsible before God for a wife and two daughters."

"My marriage is finished."

"You haven't worked at it."

"I'm in love with Betty."

"A divorcee you met at a bar. How could that be right?"

"I want to marry her."

"Son, even if your wife was dead, you're going to the wrong places to find a good woman. You'll never get a pearl in a pig sty."

Roy cooled his anger, shrugged and put on his debonair manner. "You live your life, Dad, and I'll live mine. I'll make a few wrong turns now and then, but live and learn, I say."

Betty also warded off her parents' strong objections.

"So what if he's married," she said. "Roy has stayed with his wife only for the sake of his children. He doesn't love her; he loves me."

Neither Betty nor Roy wanted any part of religion. For two years they dated while the divorce went through. Then they wed. Into the marriage Betty brought Doug and Greg, her two small sons, ages five and three. A year later their marriage produced a daughter, Crystal. Roy's former wife and two daughters moved to California.

The new marriage was soon in trouble. The evenings of dancing and drinking at bars during their courtship had been fun, Betty thought. Shortly after the wedding, she realized something: her new husband drank too much and spent too much money. Alcohol made Roy's temper flare. Quarrels began.

They decided a change in location was needed. Roy obtained a new job in a construction company, and they moved to Corpus Christi, Texas. But the marriage continued to deteriorate, based as it was on drinking, partying, distrust, jealousy and a reluctance on the part of both to face responsibility.

Next door to the Millers was a Christian couple who sensed right away that their new neighbors had deep problems. The children were often sick and cried a lot. Roy's drinking problem was obvious. This couple began praying for the Miller family.

When debts piled up, Roy came to a decision one day. "Okay, I'll compromise," he said grandly to Betty. "I'll knock off the hard liquor from now on and be strictly a beer drinker."

"That will cut down our spending a little," Betty agreed. "But we can't establish credit until we budget our money."

"I'll manage better," he promised. "And there's something else: I think we should send our kids to Sunday School."

"You want to join a church?" Betty asked doubtfully.

"No. If we send the kids to church, we'll get a free Sunday morning baby sitter."

"What church do you have in mind?"

"I don't care. The one our neighbors attend is okay. They've offered to take them each Sunday and bring them home."

Roy and Betty both agreed it was a great way to have a morning for themselves. Their neighbors began gathering up the children each Sunday morning at 9:30 and bringing them back three hours later. Betty and Roy never bothered to inquire the name of the church their children—now five, eight and 10—were attending.

Crystal began to come home each Sunday singing choruses with tender, loving messages which made Roy and Betty a bit uncomfortable. Then Doug and Greg returned one Sunday and told their parents that Jesus had come to live in their hearts.

"That's fine, Doug," Betty said indifferently. "How did it happen?"

"We knelt at the altar and prayed."

"Oh."

"Jesus loves us. It says so in the Bible."

"That's right," said Roy. "Jesus was a fine man."

"Jesus died for us. Then He went to Heaven and sent the Holy Spirit to live inside us."

"I see." Roy and Betty looked at each other uncomfortably.

"Jesus can save us from sin, you know."

"Who told you that?"

"The pastor. He prayed for us at the altar. He told us to tell you he would like to come and talk with you."

"That won't be necessary."

"He wants to invite you to come to church. Won't you come, please?"

The three children were now staring at their parents with pleading eyes.

Roy decided to end the discussion. "I learned all about religion when I was your age. It's okay, but don't take it too seriously. People with too much religion do strange things."

"Daddy, are you going to Heaven?" The plea came from Crystal whose wide eyes suddenly filled with tears.

"We'll talk about Heaven some other day," Roy said firmly. "It's time for lunch."

But the conversation haunted Roy and Betty. They didn't know that prayers were being said for them daily, not only by their neighbors but also by their own children. All they were aware of was that they felt defensive with their children and vaguely troubled for the first time about their inadequacies as parents.

Then Roy received disturbing news from his first wife. His oldest daughter, Pam, had run away from home and was last seen living in a community family in Hollywood, California. Her mother reported that she had started smoking some unusual cigarettes and using a drug she could not afford. When she began shoplifting to supplement her small allowance, she was caught. What could be done?

Roy and Betty looked at each other in bewilderment. What could they do? Invite Pam to Texas to live with them? But they had troubles enough of their own. Especially since Roy had developed an ulcer, and doctors had told him he needed an operation. This was the wrong time to add another person to their household.

But Roy's conscience was being strangely stabbed—a new experience. His daughter was in trouble; he couldn't turn his back on her. In desperation Roy and Betty visited their next-door neighbors and poured out their troubles. The neighbors—concerned, devout, compassionate—added Pam to their prayers and urged Roy to find her and bring her to Texas.

Roy did. To his surprise Pam was overjoyed to see him and willingly accompanied her father to Corpus Christi where she got a job and lived in the Miller home.

In the months that followed Roy had his operation; surgery removed two-thirds of his stomach. As he recuperated, he watched with amazement the startling developments in connection with his daughter.

First, Pam began going to church with the next-door neighbors and the three Miller children.

Second, she came back one Sunday with shining eyes to report she had surrendered her life to Jesus Christ and was a new person.

Third, she met a young man stationed at the navy base in Corpus Christi—also a Christian—and the two fell in love and asked permission to be married.

Fourth, a radiant Pam and her boyfriend were married in the church and began a new life together.

The impact of this wholesome, joyous spiritual courtship and marriage on Roy and Betty was strong. All four of their children had now become Christians and were healthier, happier and less self-centered as a result. Roy and Betty were still bogged down with the same old problems.

Roy's job called for a transfer, and he was moved to Houston. Before leaving, Roy alone went to visit their neighbors and this time asked for prayer. "Maybe with this change of job, we'll have a change of luck," he told his friends.

"Do you want God to change your circumstances or to change you?" he was asked.

Roy ducked the question. He still wasn't ready to consider the idea that he needed to change his lifestyle.

Betty was relieved when Roy went to Houston by himself to work for three weeks and look for a house. She wasn't sure she wanted to stay with Roy. Their finances were a mess. Roy was testy with the two boys; they were not his sons and he resented the money they cost him.

Meanwhile Roy's first wife called several times to report that their 14 year old, Lynn, was becoming a serious problem; she was disrespectful, refused to obey and was skipping school. Would Roy and Betty take on Lynn?

Now Betty felt trapped and desperate. Roy was still drinking and had at times been physically abusive. She wrote Roy in Houston, "We are not coming to join you. This is a convenient place for us to separate and call it quits. I'm giving up on the marriage."

At this crisis point, Roy wished his Christian neighbors were there to give him counsel. Lacking this, he looked around for the church nearest to his motel. One Sunday night he walked into ours. My husband's sermon topic was, "God Never Leads Us to a Dead End." At the close of the service Carl invited anyone who needed prayer and ministry to come forward.

A lanky, good-looking man walked down the aisle and knelt at the altar, offering 40 wasted years to God. Afterwards Roy Miller and my husband retired to Carl's office. Roy poured out his heart and asked God to deliver him from the love of alcohol and to heal his temper which had recently caused him to break furniture and push Betty around physically in anger. When I met Roy after this session with Carl, it was hard to believe that this amusing, entertaining, lovable person could have such a dual personality.

Roy called Betty that night and told her that he had surrendered his life to Jesus Christ. She accepted the news warily, feeling it was just a ploy to try and keep the marriage going. Roy started to attend our church. We soon learned that he had a good singing voice and invited him to sing in the choir. Meanwhile Carl and I had joined the prayer chain for the whole Miller family.

Several weeks later he returned to Corpus Christi to spend the weekend with his family. The first night after the children were in bed, he took his wife's hand and sat with her on the living room sofa.

"Betty, it has taken me over 40 years to make sense out of life," he said. "I've done most everything there is to do, yet nothing has brought me any real peace or satisfaction. That is until I gave my messed-up life to the Lord there in Carl Malz's church. For the first time, I think I can make it as a husband and father."

His wife struggled with conflicting emotions. Having given up on the marriage, she was reluctant to try again. Betty had lost respect for Roy and was suspicious of his new-found religion. Her Roman Catholic background made it hard for her to understand the emotionalism of born-again experiences. Despite her indifference, even hostility to the church, she had always had a vague belief in God. Her God simply hadn't been relevant to her life. Now the children and Roy were all talking a new language. She felt threatened by their prayers for her and by their brand of Christianity.

Eight years of marriage had not been kind to Betty. Her bouncy, insouciant spirit had been dampened by bickering and quarreling; heavy housework with little help had given her a washed-out look. Then there had been an unfortunate accident which had left one of her eyes badly crossed. Doctors had not been able to get it straightened. As a result she was self-conscious, less inclined to go out among people.

Betty wished her husband would take her into his arms instead of talking about Jesus Christ. She needed to know that he still loved her. Jesus seemed so remote from their lives. But Roy couldn't seem to talk about anything else.

"Jesus accepts us just as we are, Betty. That's what's so great about Him. He loves us. He forgives our sins. He will become the Head of our home. It will make all the difference—you wait and see."

Betty sighed. "I just don't know, Roy. I don't know how I feel about you anymore. I guess for the kids, I should try again. But don't insist that I believe like you do. I don't feel at all like that."

"Give it a try, Betty. Come to Houston with me, and we'll go to church there together. Will you try once more?"

She and Roy and the children came to Houston. That Sunday night as the choir was singing the opening call to worship, down the aisle marched Roy, a big grin on his face. Walking beside him was a petite, thin, but shapely young woman, tastefully dressed. As I looked closer, I noticed one of her eyes was badly crossed toward her nose. Close behind them were three unusually attractive children: two boys, Doug and Greg, approaching puberty, and seven-year-old Crystal.

At the close of the service, they waited to talk with my husband and me. When I met Betty my heart hurt with compassion. The crossed eye had increased her feelings of inferiority. I sensed that our love had brought her close to tears. Carl suggested we all kneel at the foot of the altar. Betty hesitated only for a moment. What a striking picture the five of them were as they asked Jesus to mend their family.

In the days that followed, Betty and I became friends. Since the Millers were having trouble finding a place to live, I suggested we pray for this. Because few landlords want to rent to a family with three children, the Millers knew they must buy a home. But too many debts had destroyed their credit rating, making them a poor risk for a loan.

Betty told me later that she was eating lunch alone in a restaurant one day when she felt compelled to bow her head and silently pray, "Lord, if You care, help me find a house."

After lunch Betty said she started driving back to the motel when she found herself going down a different street. One very attractive house grabbed her attention. In front of it was a man painting the front steps. On an impulse she stopped and asked if by any chance the house was for rent.

"I'm fixing it up to put it on the market," he replied.

Betty was startled by the timing of her prayer and then finding this house. She asked for special terms. Within two weeks, the deal was transacted on a contract basis.

Betty's experience with the house was another answer to our prayers. The next time she and I met I was led to pose this question.

"Have you ever asked God to straighten your eyes?"

Betty looked surprised. "The doctors gave me quite a thorough examination. An operation might do it, but that would be costly and dangerous. I'm not ready for that yet."

I didn't pursue it.

Watching the Miller family come together reminded me of a picture puzzle of the ocean my brother, Don, began putting together when we were children. When we sat down together at the kitchen table to fit the pieces together, to our disappointment we learned there were several missing. Don found similar pieces, in color and shape, from an old puzzle that we had discarded. He began to cut, scrape, and sandpaper them to the shapes needed. It was a much more difficult task than he first thought it would be, just as Roy and Betty discovered how much patience, sacrifice and time it took to glue together two broken families.

We watched it happen. The Miller children began singing in the junior choir. Betty and Roy became faithful in the adult choir. Carl spent hours with them in counseling sessions. When tempers flared they learned to stop and ask God to help them.

Lynn, Roy's younger daughter, came to join the family shortly thereafter. Almost 15, she had resented the restrictions her mother had imposed on her.

Lynn had tried to steal a car from a parking lot, and on several occasions had slipped out of the house, pushing the family car to get it away from the house before starting it. Then she would stay out until the morning hours with young friends. The Millers had a major problem on their hands.

Full of guilt because of his neglect of her when Lynn was small, Roy overdid the loving father bit at first. There wasn't anything he wouldn't do for his daughter. There are many times when Christians need to correct other Christians. This was one of them. Roy was shown how harmful his attitude was to the family as a whole. She was just one of four children and needed discipline as well as attention.

At first Lynn resisted the Miller routine of church activities and family prayers. But she was surrounded by love. Her rebellious outbursts were ignored; sometimes she had to be punished.

I'll never forget the Sunday morning when Lynn knelt at the altar of the church, asking to receive what the rest of the family had. She had been miserable the past weeks. Though the Christian life had been strange to her, she needed and wanted its peace and joy.

After her decision for the Lord, Lynn began enjoying school. She joined the youth choir and the church Bible-study group. Then she wrote back to her mother, asking forgiveness for causing her so much trouble. What a joy it was, watching that girl blossom from a bud into a rose!

Betty admitted to me one day that she was in spiritual trouble. Four children kept her busy from dawn to dusk with household work. She was jealous of Roy's lighter work load, his natural gift at entertaining people with his clowning. Other women married to somber men found Roy exciting and attractive.

I felt the Holy Spirit nudge me that behind all this was

Betty's feelings of inferiority because of her crossed eye. To take her mind off this, I urged her to concentrate on her special talents: singing, sewing, and dress designing. Then I asked her if she would make several dresses for me when I did television appearances. She did them so well she soon had work for others in the community.

We watched the Millers grow and develop a ministry of "helps." They brought to church and to their home other families with problems and were able to show them the way of happiness. Fellow employees with drinking and smoking problems began to come to Roy for help and for support in prayer.

I found another link in this prayer chain for the Millers several months later while in the home of Len and Catherine LeSourd. At dinner one night Catherine's daughter-in-law, Edith Marshall, admired the white eyelet blouse I was wearing. This led me to tell them the story of Roy and Betty Miller. "Even though her eyes are crossed she does such beautiful work."

"If God has brought such miracles to this family, He certainly wants to straighten her eyes," Len said. Then in a most conversational way he looked up and said, "Lord Jesus, You healed this woman's marriage, now we ask you to heal her crossed eyes."

Returning to my home in Texas, I told Betty the next time I saw her about the prayer for her eyes to be healed. She began to weep. "I've lived in hopes for years that someday Roy could admire my eyes again. I have almost given up."

Following the morning worship service on Sunday, Carl and I prayed with her, anointing her with oil, praying the prayer of faith that the work would be completed. She looked up and said, "I feel selfish. My brother Randy's eyes are weak and in worse shape than mine. He is younger, needs to drive a car and needs a job. I would rather you pray for his eyes."

Carl laughingly told her, "God's miracles are not short in supply. They are unending. One more miracle won't bankrupt God or short change anyone else." Betty bowed her head and prayed, "Oh Jesus, our great Physician, heal my brother Randy's eyes."

The following Thursday, her brother Randy called her from Milwaukee, Wisconsin. "Sis, a mysterious thing has happened. My eyes are suddenly so much better. I took a driver's test and passed. So I've bought myself a new car, some new clothes and applied for a position as a social worker on the campus of the University of Wisconsin. Today I got the job!" Randy had earned a master's degree and was a qualified social worker, but his eyes had always held him back.

How beautiful is the rippling effect of Christ's power as it permeates a family through prayer, starting with one or two and then spreading ever outward, touching children, grandchildren, parents, grandparents, in-laws, aunts, uncles, nieces and nephews.

A few months later we moved from Texas to South Dakota. When I said good-by to Betty, I felt a pang of disappointment. Her brother's eyes had been healed, but hers were still crossed. Several weeks later she called to tell me with some excitement that she had felt a pulling sensation in her bad eye, and there had been a definite improvement.

In September came another excited report by telephone. Betty and Roy had spent the entire day raking leaves and working in the yard. Late in the afternoon she had leaned against Roy to prop herself up. He suddenly exclaimed, "Betty your eyes are straight! Go look in the mirror!"

"It was true," she told me excitedly. "They are straight."

At Thanksgiving I received a long distance phone call from my friend, Jeanette Dunkerson, who verified the healing. She had met Betty in the grocery store and was astonished that her eyes were straight. "We honestly could not tell or remember which eye had been so badly crossed."

The Lord still has much work to do with the Miller family, but what a way they have come. On Christmas morning that year Betty found a poem from her 10-year-old Greg which he placed in her Bible. It read:

Christmas

Christmas used to be a regular thing,
No Christmas songs would we sing.
We never prayed before we ate,
The joy of Christmas wasn't so great.

The Christmas Spirit was kind of gloomy and gray,
We didn't celebrate it as Christ's birthday.
Mom and Dad, now you are really God's Chosen People.
Now you don't go to bars, you go to the good House with
the steeple.

We even have happy Christian meetings,
This poem is my Son-to-Parents greetings.
I can't say anything more
Except that I love you both, more than I ever did before.

By Greg

12

PRAYER WARRIORS

THERE IS ONE type of prayer which we should be using more and more in our tumultuous world as the forces of good and evil collide. When we get involved in spiritual warfare, we know we need the "whole armor of God" to protect us and our loved ones. In the sixth chapter of Ephesians Paul describes this "armor" in detail (Ephesians 6:11–20), urging Christians to take "the sword of the Spirit, which is the Word of God. Pray at all times in the Spirit . . ." (TLB).

In effect, we are urged to become "prayer warriors" in order to cope with the forces of evil.

My first encounter with a genuine "prayer warrior" came when I was at a young, impressionable age. My Uncle Cecil, a U.S. Air Corps pilot, was shot down in combat in World War II. He was seriously injured when he crash-landed the plane in England; the control stick ran through his stomach and groin.

The moment a cablegram brought the news, I heard my parents, with one voice, say, "Call old Warhorse Buckland!"

The call was placed to a country house located north of South Bend, Indiana, near the Michigan border. Two days later we got word that Uncle Cecil had regained consciousness and would recover. He then went on to make a career in the Air Force, is now retired and serving on the advisory board of Douglas Aircraft.

Months later a distraught woman knocked on the door of our house one night, awakening our entire family. When my father opened the door she almost fell into his arms. "Ralph has gone wild again, Pastor. Please call the police."

Instead of calling the police my Dad put on his overcoat and barked an order to mother, "Call old Warhorse Buckland!"

I don't know what happened other than that my father had a long session with the woman and her demented husband—plus the prayers of "old Warhorse Buckland." Two Sundays later Ralph came to the altar after church and accepted Jesus as his personal Savior. In the years that followed Ralph was a loving husband, responsible parent and a resourceful citizen of the community.

What a powerhouse the "Old Warhorse" must be! The day finally came to which we had so looked forward. "Old Warhorse Buckland" was coming to our house for dinner. We children (I was about 10) could hardly wait. I envisioned him as a seven-foot giant of a man, with broad chest, booming voice and flashing eyes who might even ride to our house on a large black horse.

"Old Warhorse" arrived in a small car. Dad hurried down to the street to help *her* out of the back seat and up the porch steps. She tottered a bit from old age. She was small-boned, small in size and plainly dressed.

I was terribly let down until I looked into her face. Graying hair framed strong angular features: firm, resolute chin, high cheekbones, patrician nose, character lines creasing her forehead like rivulets. But it was her eyes that held me. Sunk deep into her head, they flashed determination, tenacity, power. Flecks of fire seemed to emanate from the gray irises of her eyes.

I trembled when she took my hand, but her voice was not sharp; it was almost gentle. She so inspired my confidence that I asked her how she got her prayer power.

Out came the story of her life. As a girl she was plain, with no special gifts. She couldn't sing, play an instrument or use her hands skillfully with knitting and sewing. She was too small to engage in sports. But she did love to read.

Stories of courage fascinated her. She fantasized about riding horses to battle. As an American Joan of Arc, she vanquished the forces of evil in every battle. When she became an all-out believer, she transferred her battles to the spiritual realm. And then came the discovery: God had given her the gift of prayer power for others!

The label "Old Warhorse" came soon afterwards. She figuratively rode horses to battle as she fought the forces of Satan. Her prayers were not loud; they were intense, prolonged—in fact, unceasing. As she prayed for people in crisis, she put on the whole armor of God, claimed the power of Jesus, mounted her horse and went against "the rulers, the authorities, against the powers of this dark world and against the spiritual forces of evil in the heavenly realms."

"Old Warhorse" didn't need to leave her house to wage her battles. When Uncle Cecil was near death, she called upon ministering angels to come to his aid and even though he was thousands of miles away in a foreign hospital, I'm convinced that the heavenly host responded to the call from "Warhorse Buckland."

The demons that possessed Ralph didn't have a chance against "Old Warhorse." She took authority, called for the warrior angels, and Ralph was delivered. This "little" woman does not stop her prayer when the enemy is in retreat. She keeps praying after the victory is won, only too aware that the enemy will return if given a chance. Too many victories have turned into defeats, she maintains, because the celebrating people let down their defenses.

Another such prayer warrior is Thelma Atkinson. When her husband died (Delbert Atkinson had been the mayor of Pasadena, Texas), Thelma discovered she had a gift of the "ministry of helps," which is assisting others by prayer to do what they could not do on their own. Not an outgoing woman, Thelma quietly began teaching a Sunday School class and instructing a women's group in prayer.

Through the Holy Spirit she got a nudge every time I was in some kind of trouble. I cannot explain this, only that God reveals things to people who are sensitive to Him and to others. I never hinted to her that I had a need, but twice she sent me money when there was an outstanding expense facing us. On several occasions she phoned to tell me that she had prayed for me at a certain time; in each case there had been a crisis situation which had been resolved in an almost supernatural way.

Once I was wrestling with how to tell Heather's story in Chapter 7. I struggled for weeks, several times wondering if I shouldn't just drop it. There was deep, inner conflict inside me.

The telephone rang early one morning. "Betty, I was awakened at 4:30 A.M. by the sound of your voice calling me. I slid out of bed onto my knees and swung a two-edged sword of prayer for you against forces that want to confuse you. Stand firm on what it is you are trying to do."

I thanked her and told her the problem.

"I'll be your 'spiritual bodyguard' until you work through it," she promised.

What wonderful gifts "Old Warhorse" and Thelma have, and how they are needed today. We know we receive help from the heavenly host, but spiritual bodyguards and prayer warriors are essential to ring the alarm bells and call out the unseen allies. The key to their power is that they have learned to pray in the Spirit.

When I face something very crucial and feel that I must get through to the Lord, I find a quiet place alone with God. Then I begin to praise and worship Him until I feel the warmth of His presence. Sometimes I repeat this key verse: "Likewise the Spirit also helpeth our infirmities: for we know not what we should pray for as we ought: but the Spirit itself maketh intercession for us with groanings which cannot be uttered. And he that searcheth the hearts knoweth what is the mind of the Spirit, because He maketh intercession for the saints according to the will of God" (Romans 8:26,27).

The prayer warriors penetrate a barrier here that brings them to the higher reaches. The indwelling Spirit within them takes over and "maketh intercession" with Almighty God for the person desperately ill or the one in trouble.

When I pray through such a barrier it's almost as though I go into overdrive, and my words come out in a language which I do not understand. By praying this way, since the words can't usually be understood except by God, they cannot be intercepted by the enemy—and the answer can't be blocked.

After I have prayed in this way, I usually feel a release, a surge of trust and hope. I have prayed through. And I am through. If, after committing anything to God, I can come away with my mind lifted, then I have prayed through in faith.

Prayer warfare is hard work, entirely different from "believing for" something where only you and God are involved. It takes more time. It involves a call to all the heavenly forces. And the work is not all verbalized prayer or intense listening. So often the door to answered prayer is opened by the Word. Thus a prayer warrior has to value the Bible as a handbook of life. He must know it so well he can pour out large sections of it by heart.

An incident during our move from Texas to South Dakota confirmed this point for me. April and I were driving the Ramcharger, pulling the trailer containing our mare and colt. In Dallas, we were to take "35W northwest." This turn-off is famous for being hard to find. As we approached the city, a sudden, near-hurricane wind-squall of rain hit us.

Hailstones pelted down on the truck and metal trailer, frightening the mare; I can't even imagine what this awesome noise did to that two-week-old colt. We missed the turn-off and suddenly were in downtown Dallas with six freeways running all about us. Since I was pulling a trailer for the first time in my life, when I realized we were in a location where it was prohibited, I nearly panicked.

"Why not use the CB radio?" April suggested. "Someone will tell us what to do."

I nodded and reached for the mike but with deep uncertainty. I had never bothered to read the handbook for the operation of a CB radio. Helplessly I looked at the dials.

"Turn it to Channel 19, Mother," said April.

I did so, then picked up the mike and said uncertainly, "I'm driving to South Dakota and missed my turn. Can someone help me get onto highway 35W?"

April shook her head as I listened to a confusion of talk and static on the set. "Mother, you're going at it wrong. You're not talking to a ladies luncheon; they're truckers out there. You gotta talk their language. May I try it?"

I gave her the mike, and she took a deep breath.

"Breaker 19," she said crisply, "for a radio check . . . "

A deep, booming bass voice came back, "Radio check . . . how mucha puttin' down?"

" 'Bout seven—maybe 10."

"What's your 10–20?" the deep voice came back.

"We're lost. We've got a horse trailer, and the horses are goin' *crazeeee;* gotta git to Dakotas. How 'bout some help gettin' through Dallas goin' north—need to get to 35W."

I stared at April in amazement. Was this my sweet, gentle 12-year-old who had such an angelic singing voice? Where had she picked up that lingo?

The booming bass came back. "This here's the Black Panther from the Texas Panhandle. I spot you. Turn around at next exit. Go back three miles. Whatcher handle, good buddy?"

"This here's the Dakota Kid," returned April in a somewhat twangy voice, I thought.

"Good luck, Dakota Kid, little buddy. Ten-four, over and out and through!"

When we were back on course, I asked her, "April Dawn, where did you learn that kind of talk?"

"Mother, we tried to get you to read the handbook. Daddy

spent good money to buy that CB dictionary. I read it. When you know the words, you can get the help."

As we drove north, I thanked God for the reminder. To perform almost any job in the world, we have a special handbook which tells us what to do and how to do it. If we don't follow the instructions, we are soon in trouble. When occasions arise where we must battle the forces of darkness, God has provided us the handbook we need containing His Word. I need to use it every day to stay in spiritual shape.

If I had to depend solely upon my own resources to make it in this world, I would fail. I am an ordinary, weak human being. But thank God, I don't have to depend on my human methods to win my battles. I use God's mighty weapons, not those made by men, to knock down the devil's strongholds. These weapons can break down every proud argument, penetrate the strongholds of stubborn will, intellectual reasoning, negative thinking, sin and crime. God's weapon through prayer can break down every wall that can be built to keep men from finding Him. With His weapons, we can capture rebels and bring them back to God. That scripture is a powerful "10–4, over, out and through good buddy," as the CBers would say (2 Corinthians 10:4, TLB, paraphrased).

I'm not talking about the prayers of praise, heart prayers, simple prayers of faith where all involved are believers in God. When we begin to pray for an evil or lost person and come against the "powers and principalities," then it becomes spiritual warfare. Then prayer needs to have a cutting edge like a laser beam.

I had just fallen asleep one Wednesday night when I felt a soft paw on my elbow. It was our mother cat, Curious, reminding me that I had forgotten to put her out so she could haunt the red barn for mice all night. Quietly I crept down to the front door and let her out, hoping not to wake the other members of my family.

I was on my way back to bed when the phone rang. I

grabbed it and stretching the 13-foot cord to its full length, took the phone into the dark bathroom nearby and shut the door before saying, "Hello."

"Is your name Malz?" asked the operator. "I have a party on the line who keeps repeating 'Malz, Malz.' You are the only Malz listed in this area. It is a long distance call and will have to be collect. Will you pay?"

"Yes, I will accept that call." I told her.

The voice was faint. "I have swallowed two bottles of sleeping pills. I'm sick. I'm dizzy. I'm afraid. I wish I hadn't done it. Pray to God for me."

"What's wrong?" I stammered.

"I've cheated on my husband. My lover won't marry me. It's over."

"Where are you?"

"I don't know. In a hotel room. It's the end, but I don't want to go to hell. I read your book and decided to call you. Please pray for me."

"You must pray too," I almost shouted. "Ask God to forgive you and be merciful to you . . ."

Then I heard the phone click. She had hung up. Frantically, I dialed the operator. She said there was no way to trace the call.

"Oh God," I cried out as I slumped onto the floor of the bathroom, my nose pressed against the cold tiles in my helplessness. "God, have mercy on this poor soul. You are everywhere. You know where this woman is. Don't let her die. Forgive her for trying to take her life. Don't let the sleeping pills have any effect; cancel their action!"

I fought and warred; I battled and groaned, hurting down deep in my groin, like I was having labor pains. Then I prayed in the Spirit, groanings only God would understand. "Old Warhorse" Buckland had been dead many years, but I called for her help. I pleaded for the ministering angels, the warrior angels, the guardian angels to come to this woman's aid.

While lying there on the bathroom floor in darkness, I

saw a picture of an auburn-haired, young woman, slumping
off the side of the bed, her hair tousled, her arms dangling
lifelessly. Then the picture changed, and her head was not
descending onto the floor but was being drawn upright, and
her body was being sucked upward at an unbelievable pace
of speed. I heard the thundering of hoofs and saw a gar-
rison of horrible-looking black horses, on whose backs rode
leering, evil-looking, half-men, half-beast riders. They
were circling the auburn-haired woman as she plunged toward a planet of fire. The horses then melded together in
a black funnel which pointed into the fiery mass. There were
hideous screams. When the woman cringed to protect
her face from the heat, I put my arms over my head
too.

I breathed four words: *The blood of Jesus.*

Then came what was like the roll of heavy waves dashing
upon the beach, followed by a flash of white light. The light
turned into whirling white forms, thousands of them, hurling
themselves on the dark funnel, splintering the blackness into
many thousands of fragments.

The direction of the woman changed. Instead of her reddish hair flowing wildly above her head, the hair settled
around her shoulders. The anguish in her face was gone,
and her body sped back the way it had come with unbelievable
speed.

The battle had gone on for a long time—an hour or more.
Now came a sudden inner peace and with it the words of
an old hymn I hadn't heard in years:

> In the midst of battle be thou not dismayed,
> Though the powers of darkness 'gainst thee are arrayed;
> God thy strength is with thee, causing thee to stand,
> Heaven's allied armies wait at thy command.
>
> Victory! victory! blessed blood bought victory!
> Victory! victory! victory all the time;
> As Jehovah liveth, strength divine He giveth
> Unto those who know Him, victory all the time.

I sat up, weak but relieved. The battle was over. The heavenly forces had turned the tide. I knew that woman would live, would find peace and there would be no mental damage from the two bottles of sleeping pills.

The call had come on a Wednesday night. I was playing the organ the following Sunday night at the church when about halfway through the service I glanced up from my music to see a young, attractive, red-haired woman walk down the aisle alone. I had never met the woman before but I had seen her! She sat down about a third of the way from the back of the sanctuary and removed her mink cape.

Carl began his sermon. My mind was churning and drifted away from his words several times. Then my husband said, "I read an account of a Baptist minister who was almost paralyzed with grief when his only daughter ran away from home. He was too proud to tell anyone. He prayed in agony and desperation until he felt that he had broken through to God. Then several weeks later, his daughter returned.

"She told her father an unusual story: 'I was sitting in my car, trying to get it to start. Something had gone wrong with the ignition. I was distressed. Nothing was going right for me. I did not have the money for automobile repairs. I started to cry; then I prayed that if the Lord would get this car to start, I would return home, ask forgiveness and try to help my father in his church work. On the very next try, the car started.'"

Carl then pushed aside his notes and spoke earnestly: "If anyone here has fled from parents or husband or wife—or turned your back on God—please reconsider. Kneel right there in your pew or come down front to the altar. We will all pray together and ask for forgiveness. Then I urge you to return to your family; return your soul and heart to God."

I moved over to the organ and began to play the invitation song:

> I wandered far away from God;
> Now I'm coming home.
> The path of sin, too long I've trod;
> Lord, I'm coming home.

I saw the auburn-haired woman slip out of her seat and walk toward the back door. "Lord, stop her," I whispered. "Holy Spirit, wrap your loving, forgiving arms around her and bring her back!"

She hesitated, closed the door, returned to the pew where she had been sitting and knelt. I stopped playing and rushed quickly to her side and knelt with her. Whispering so that no one could hear, I asked, "Did you call me Wednesday night?"

She began to sob uncontrollably, "Yes."

"I knew it!" I told her, "How much God must love you to give you a second chance to live."

"How did your husband know?" she sobbed. "My dad was a Baptist minister, too."

We prayed together. I could almost see joy and life return to her eyes.

After everyone else had left, she told us what had happened. After taking the two bottles of sleeping pills and calling, she passed out. Then came a horrible nightmare. When she awoke the following afternoon she could not believe she was still alive. She was a little drowsy, but after ordering a pot of coffee and a glass of milk from room service, she checked out of the hotel and drove back to her home which was not far from our church. On Sunday night she felt a compelling urge to come to our service but had no intention of admitting to me that she was my Wednesday night caller.

I've kept in touch with her for the past five years. She terminated the affair, took a new interest in her husband and three children, and is now keeping the books for her husband's business. The Lord is blessing her home.

Whenever I feel helpless, inadequate and even defeated by life, I remember people like Ruth, Marcia, the Millers and the nameless, auburn-haired woman. Their lives were transformed through the power of God which was activated by the prayers of just ordinary persons like myself. I am awed that the Lord sees fit to use us as His instruments in the fulfilling of His Master Plan.

13

THE LEFT HAND OF GOD

SOME WHO READ to this point will say, "Betty, I have a question. At times my prayers seem to go unanswered. I wonder if God even hears them. The focus of your book is on prayers that *are* answered."

And so I must tell the story of my cousin's daughter. Angela was a golden-haired, joyous child of seven, the light and life of every one of our family get-togethers. One Sunday she was staying with her grandparents, my Uncle Jesse and Aunt Gertrude. During the church service she laid her head on her grandfather's lap, complaining that her throat was sore.

At lunch Angela listlessly picked at her food. Afterwards she seemed glad to go to bed for a rest. Uncle Jesse called his son, Ken, and daughter-in-law, Louretta, and they decided to leave Angela with her grandparents for an extra day.

When Angela was no better on Monday morning, they took her to the doctor's office. The nurse took her temperature, then became alarmed. Angela's face was turning blue. A doctor was summoned who quickly observed that the glottis in Angela's throat had swollen so tight it had closed the throat and trachea, preventing breathing.

An emergency tracheotomy was performed right there in the doctor's office. Afterwards she was rushed to the hospital where a team of doctors worked for two hours to save her while all of us maintained a prayer vigil.

163

Angela died on the operating table. Her ailment was diagnosed as an acute bacteria infection, epiglotitis.

Uncle Jesse stormed at Heaven. "We can't live without this child," he wailed. "She was the brightest spot in our lives—our only grandchild."

Upon hearing the news, I felt like someone had socked me hard in the stomach. While searching the Bible for comfort I came across this verse in Isaiah:

The righteous man perishes . . . devout men are taken away, while no one understands. For the righteous [are] taken away from calamity.

Isaiah 57:1 (RSV)

That Angela's death might have spared her from something even worse was of some consolation. I also found a children's story in Mark 10:13–16. Jesus said, "Suffer [permit] the little children to come unto Me, and forbid them not: for of such is the kingdom of God." On earth, Jesus enjoyed having the children with Him. Perhaps Jesus also meant for us not to forbid Him, or be angry with Him when He took a small child in death. It is believed that we remain forever the same age we enter that place. Just as a child blesses a home, Heaven will be a more exciting place with small children around. It would not sparkle as much if everyone there arrived only after they had become old.

God knows best whether His children belong in this world or the next. We are to trust His overruling, practical, superintending providence. God is more interested in answering my need than answering my request. Sometimes because of my importunity, He may answer my request without even touching my need.

Aunt Gertrude called me a few weeks after Angela's death. "What shall I do," she asked, "with all this left-over love I have for our only grandchild? What will we do with her left-over pony, her left-over Irish setter, her left-over bedroom full of left-over toys and beautiful, left-over clothes?"

"Let's make it a matter of prayer," I suggested. "Perhaps there is some left-over child who needs it all."

A few days later, on Saturday morning, when most tykes are watching cartoons, Uncle Jesse and Aunt Gertrude heard a faint knock on the door. Opening it, they saw a tiny, frail, eight-year-old girl with long brown hair forming a tangled frame around her angelic face and two gentle blue eyes. They gasped, blinking, thinking it a mirage: the striking resemblance (except for the hair color) to the granddaughter, Angela, was too much, almost haunting!

Seeing that she had waded through more than a foot of snow in worn sneakers, they invited her in to get warm and to dry her stockings.

"I'm Nancy. I want to sing for you. Then can I shovel the snow off your porch for some money?" she asked.

After drinking a cup of hot chocolate, she shoveled the porch and was paid for it. She noticed Aunt Gertrude baking cookies and asked to stay and help. When they realized it was dusk, they suggested that they drive her home. But she replied sweetly, "I love you folks. I don't want to ever leave here."

They called her mother to ask permission to have her stay for dinner and meet Angela's grieving parents. During the conversation with Nancy's mother, they learned that the father was dead and the mother, with the help of welfare aid, was trying to stay home and, as best she could, hold the family of eight children together. The oldest was 14.

As they started to eat, Angela's parents, Ken and "Retta," dropped in to say hello on their way home. They were astonished when they saw the child, Nancy, sitting where Angela used to sit at the table.

Now, months later, she is still there. She has become the grandchild and child replacement for both the homes. They discovered that she had some left-over talent. With Aunt Gertrude's piano accompaniment, she is singing some of the same songs that their daughter sang before leaving for college. Nancy sang two solos at church recently. She goes home to visit her seven brothers and sisters about once a week.

Each Sunday morning, Aunt Gertrude loads up her car with all eight of those children and takes them to church with her.

When any "Angela" dies, there will always be a "Nancy" needing left-over love. Angela will never die as long as a Nancy can be found. Love will never die as long as there are grandparents like my Uncle Jesse and Aunt Gertrude.

When my husband went in for heart surgery in 1965, two people came to pray for him and prophesied that he would recover and live a full life. He died in the hospital.

With a broken heart but an open mind, I groped for an answer in the Bible.

I read: "For my thoughts are not your thoughts, neither are your ways my ways, saith the Lord. For as the heavens are higher than the earth, so are my ways higher than your ways, and my thoughts than your thoughts" (Isaiah 55:8,9). Our plans are short-term earth plans; His are long-range eternal, unending programming.

I received a letter recently from my first mother-in-law, Dorothy Upchurch. For more than 13 years she has felt some resentment toward me for allowing her son, John, to go ahead with the heart surgery that resulted in his death. She questioned these long years why God did not answer her mother's heartfelt prayer and heal him.

Dear Betty,

When Johnnie first died, I suffered from disappointed shock.

Many years I've spent in grieving. I fell before God, continually praying for a personal revelation from God to me, telling me where John was. I had to be sure. I believed he was a good man, loving you and attending church. But only God really knows the heart.

Then I had a dream or vision. I do not know if I was awake or asleep. I only know it was divine and it was real. I saw a great, vast multitude of people. I was sitting at a magnificent table. The banquet guests including myself were talking in the atmosphere of great joy, when suddenly out of the masses of jubilant voices, I recognized one voice that I would know anywhere, on earth or in Heaven. It was John. He spoke only one word: "Mama!" I turned to see him in that great redeemed throng of saints, robed in white transparent raiment that glowed and glistened with God's light and life eternal. His face shone with a smile of overcoming victory.

Now, Betty, you can be sure I am happy, knowing where he is. I pray that his daddy and I, along with his sister Helen, and brothers, Stan and Herschel, will all be rejoined with him around the throne of God.

Love and prayers,
Mom Upchurch (Dorothy)

Mother Upchurch received an answer to her prayer for an understanding of death, and it was beautiful.

We can go to the Bible as an unfailing source of help. In the book that bears his name, Job never did understand why he went through the great trials that he did: the destruction of his home, death of children, the drought, the loss of his fortune. But he trusted God and reverenced the gap between the things he did and did not understand. Eventually God rewarded him with twice as much of everything that he had before.

My new husband, Carl, has given me a new insight in understanding the seemingly unanswered prayer. He feels that too little is said about the "left hand of God." God has two hands, yet we hear of only the one, His right hand, the hand of power, immediate deliverance and protection.

It takes the pressure of two hands to mold a vessel. It takes two hands to make a man or woman who is to be of special use to God. We want miracles; God wants us to be the miracle of His making. We want charisma; He wants to mold our character. We want anointing; He gives us agony, knowing that nothing great is produced without suffering. Even Jesus learned obedience through suffering. We want providence to deliver us; He subjects us to a scraping process in order to perfect us.

God has two hands: the right hand for miracles and the left hand for molding. Both are His hands, and both convey His loving touch.

God does answer every prayer. We either get the answer we want, or the answer He wants; but answer He does. Job said, "The Lord giveth and the Lord taketh away. Blessed be the name of the Lord." Job was convinced that his loss was not the result of foolishness or sin. He prayed about the circumstance. He learned then as we do now: If it is God who takes, He always gives in return.

During my death and out-of-the-body experience, I stood in His presence and witnessed prayer in the form of direct, pulsating shafts of light, joining the great light in Heaven's throne room. I am confident of the power of prayer. Since then, when I stand or kneel in prayer I feel that same power and know that there is not unbridgable distance between earth and Heaven—from man to God. I have seen the other end of prayer. We may stand on earth and pray in faith and confidence believing that the answer will come.